ABHINANDAN H PATIL

Essential Skills for Software Engineers

Dedicated to my Family, Well wishers and Teachers

Contents

Preface

Targeted readers of this book are mostly **new entrants** in software industry. Or under graduates who want to make it to the software industry. This book should serve as starting point for them and should give them broad picture of what is what. While the Author does not claim **"Know it all"**, he makes an attempt to document his own understanding in this book. The book should serve as reference book of reference books. This book contains curated pointers for further study. The book intentionally touches too many topics while not getting into murky details of the topics. That is intentional again. If you have gone through all of by blogs , then there is no need to own this book separately.

Acknowledgement

Author acknowledges Reedsy for great documentation software.

I

General Skills of Software Engineer

This part is dedicated to general skills required by the software engineer to carry out day to day activity

1

Introduction

I will be taking rather unconventional approach in this book. Software Engineers these days have their own portfolio web sites. For example mine is at https://abhinandanhpatil.info. Quick look reveals few skills listed in the web site. And they are as follows

Eng. Abhinandan H. Patil, M. Tech, PhD (IJSER), ISTQB-CTAL-TM, CSM, SMIEEE, PMI-PMP, UGC-NET, Indian Achiever 2021-2022

Academic and Research Profile:

For Academic and Research related details, kindly visit https://abhinandan hpatil.info/about-me/

I can work as Architect or Manager for:

· Scientific Software Projects involving Mathematics
· Analytics, Data Science and Machine Learning Projects involving Python/Julia.
· System Software Projects involving C++ and Go
· Software Development in Testing Projects of Any Complexity.

Professional Summary:

I have well rounded 18.5 years (11.5 Industry + 7 Research) of experience in software development and testing with exposure to latest digital transformative technologies including Cloud, Data Science, ML/DL, Internet of Things, latest wireless network technologies, Blockchain(concepts).

My Resume Directory Link

I am a Software Generalist with exposure to multiple technologies. Exposed to latest digital transformative technologies such as AI/ML, Data Science, IoT, Cloud Computing, Block-Chain Concepts. Also well versed with traditional software engineering such as Web Technologies.

My Domain knowledge includes: Web technologies, Data Science, Machine Learning, Internet of Things, Cloud Computing, Computational Mathematics.

My Computational Mathematics Skills: Sound knowledge of Engineering Mathematics. Well versed with open source software for Computational Mathematics such as Sympy, Scipy, SAGE, Octave to name a few.

My software skills are: C, C++,Python , Go, Java,, JavaScript, Julia,, Algorithms and Data Structures, Linux, IDEs, Shell programming, Cloud, Version Control, Code Review, Coding Standards, Maintainable Code.

My ML/DL/DS Skills are as follows: Machine learning with emphasis on Mathematics specifically, Linear Algebra, Multivariate Calculus, Statistics and Probability. Abhinandan knows Scikit learn, Spark, Keras, TensorFlow, Pytorch. Visual Programming with JASP, Orange3 and Deep Learning Studio.

My SDET Skills: I can develop/maintain proprietary Automation Tools using JavaScript, Python, Java, C++, Go. I know Test Management, Monitoring/Control, Test Implementation, Execution and Reporting. For Web Testing I have used TestCafeStudio, TestCafe, JMeter, SonarQube, Clover, Junit, TestNG, Selenium, Appium, Postman, Cucumber, Gherkin. Well Versed with many Test Management and Test Execution Tools.

My Backend skills: Spring boot , Go, Microservices, Express(Nodejs), NoSQL (Mongo DB), SQL {PostgreSQL, MSSQL, MySQL}. Data formats {JSON, XML}

My Frontend skills: HTML5, CSS3, Svelte, Bootstrap, Vue3, JavaScript, Nuxt3(Learning).

I also possess brief knowledge of **Salesforce platform and MuleSoft anypoint platform.**

Programming language on the wish list of learning radar : Rust

My Preferences for Industry Projects:

- **Scientific Software Projects involving Mathematics**
- **Analytics, Data Science and Machine Learning Projects:** Julia/Python.
- **System Software Projects:** C++ 17/20 and Go
- **Software Development in Testing Projects:** Python for green field projects. Fine with JAVA projects too.

How to read this? It is mix of many skills listed in one place. This is where the Books comes handy. This Book is meant for understanding this kind of profile for newbies!. The Book therefore revolves around this topic and book is structured around it. You will find chapters on but not limited to:

Preface

Acknowledgement

GENERAL SKILLS OF SOFTWARE ENGINEER

Introduction

Mathematics and Statistics for Software Engineers

Computer Systems

Software Quality Assurance

Scripting

Choice of Operating Systems for Software Development

Traditional Programming Languages such as Assembly, C, C++

Rust and Golang

Java, Scala, Kotlin Programming Language

JavaScript as Programming Language

Python Programming Language

Visual Programming

Databases

Utilities

Data Structure and Algorithms

Data Formats

Data Analytics and Data Science

Scientific software

Design Tools

Productivity Tools

Project Specific Tools

WEB DEVELOPMENT AND WEB TESTING

Web Development and Mobile App Development

Web and Mobile Testing

SOFTWARE ARCHITECTURE AND DESIGN

Software Architecture and Design

MACHINE LEARNING AND DEEP LEARNING

Introduction to Machine Learning and Deep Learning

State of the Art of Machine Learning and Deep Learning

Selected Content from https://14inc.ltd/blog-feed/

INTERNET OF THINGS

Internet of Things

CLOUD FROM USER'S PERSPECTIVE

Cloud from Users Perspective

BLOCK CHAIN

Block Chain

Blockchain and its Applications

PROCESS RELATED

What is Process in Software Industry

DEVOPS

DevOPs

MICROCONTROLLERS AND HARDWARE

MicroControllers and Electronics

ROBOTICS

Robotics

INDUSTRY 4.0

Industry 4.0

QUANTUM COMPUTING

Quantum Computing

SUN RISE SECTORS

SUN Rise or Promising Sectors

INTANGIBLE SKILLS
Valuable Assets aka Intangible Skills
Conclusion
About the Author

Targeted readers of this book are mostly new entrants in software industry. Or under graduates who want to make it to the software industry. This book should serve as starting point for them and should give them broad picture of what is what. Author makes an attempt to document his own understanding in this book. The book should serve as reference book. The book intentionally touches too many topics while not getting into murky details of the topics. That is intentional again.

The book should give birds view of many topics. Each topic serves as the pointer using which other intricacies can be fetched. In this era of YouTube, visual learning avenues the book still attempts to take text approach for its own reason. The Author makes an attempt to explain it all in 10,000 words.

2

Mathematics and Statistics for Software Engineers

T his chapter is for software engineers working for scientific software or engineers making use of Machine Learning. Machine Learning understanding improves a lot if you are comfortable with Linear Algebra, Calculus, Probability and Statistics. One can study Mathematics in isolation or try to apply the concepts to field of study. The former can be called pure mathematics and the latter is applied. But it only makes sense when pure is applied!!

Let us take a look at the Mathematics from purists perspective. Let us look at text **book [1]** It consists of

- Sets
- Relations and Functions
- Trigonometric Functions
- Mathematical induction
- Complex numbers and quadratic equation
- Linear Inequalities
- Permutation and Combination
- Bionomial Theorem
- Sequence and Series

- Straight lines
- Conic sections
- Three dimensional geometry
- Limits and Derivatives
- Mathematical Reasoning
- Statistics
- Probability
- Inverse trigonometric functions
- Matrices
- Determinants
- Continuity and Differentiablity
- Application of Derivatives
- Integrals
- Differential equations
- Vector Algebra
- Linear programming

The same subject, Mathematics from John Birds perspective i,.e **Reference [3]**

- Numbers and Algebra
- Further numbers and algebra
- Areas and Volume
- Graphs
- Geometry and Trigonometry
- Complex Numbers
- Matrices and Determinants
- Vector geometry
- Differential calculus
- Integral calculus
- Differential equations
- Statistics and probability
- Laplace transforms
- Fourier series

- Z-transforms

Now let us look at the References. They form the spectrum. Moving from generic Mathematics to specific topic.

Broadly speaking, the Mathematics that we have to study for Machine Learning can be categorized into the following:

1. Equations, Graphs and Functions
2. Linear Algebra with emphasis on Vectors and Matrices
3. Multi-variable calculus
4. Statistics and Probability

One may argue that these are parts of software packages that we use and learning the mentioned topics is optional. Not true.

Now let us take a case study where Mathematics and Statistics are applied to real word problem and an attempt is made to understand software system using the Mathematics and Statistics. Let us look at the Journal Article "Regression Test Suite Execution Time Analysis using Statistical Techniques" [10].

Now let us try to understand what the Author of the paper is trying to say:

- He visualises the test setup as layers.
- Where top most layer is test suite
- He visualises Java Virtual Machine + Tool as next layer
- The lower most layer is Operating System + Hardware

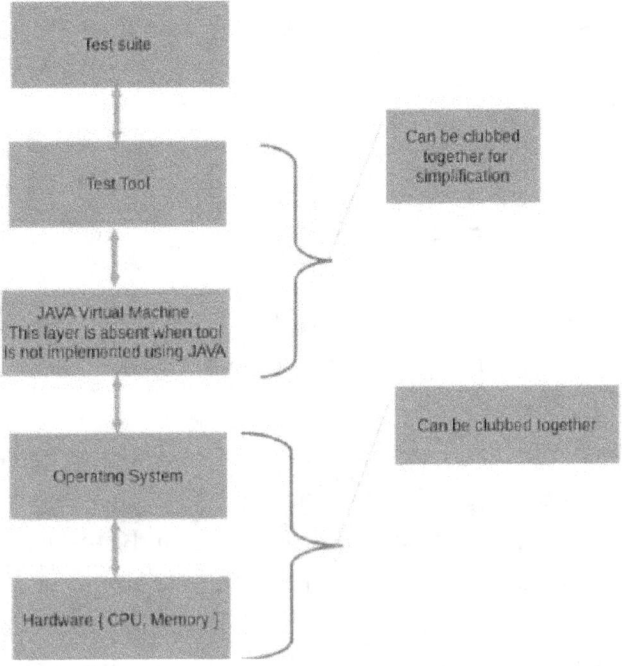

Multi Layered Test Setup

What the Author is saying is, Total execution of test case can be expressed as

F(x,y,z)

where x is due to test suite itself, y is due to JVM + Tool code and z is OS + hardware combination.

This is multi variable calculus function is characteristic of the test setup.

Further Author says that the same test case when executed multiple times, gives slightly different execution time. This is due to randomness introduced mainly due to JVM.

In quest to characterise test execution time as mathematical function, following things need to be done.

· Collection and Classification of Data
· Analytics on the Collected Data
· Representation and Visualisation of Data

If we have sufficient data points, the test execution time will be as follows:

$$y = \frac{1}{\sigma\sqrt{2\Pi}} \, e^{\frac{(x-\mu)^2}{2\sigma^2}}$$

Probability Distribution Function

Where x is individual test case execution time, and Mu and Rho are mean and standard deviation respectively. Please note that since test case execution can take continuous values and the distribution of the test case is stochastic in nature, it leads to normal distribution. This is one way of representation of test execution. The other way is characterisation of the test execution time using Analytics or **machine learning** and coming up with characteristic equation. The paper leaves it as future work.

The other important thing that paper discusses is JVM tuning parameter and its effect on the execution time.

SI No	XX Numeric option value		Test case execution time				
	x	$X = x - \bar{x}$	y	$Y = y - \bar{y}$	X^2	Y^2	XY
1							
2							
.							
.							
N							

Coefficient of correlation $= \dfrac{\Sigma XY}{\sqrt{\Sigma X^2 Y^2}}$

Correlation Table between Test Execution and JVM option

From this table one can make out how the JVM tuning numeric value is correlated to test execution time.

Why the paper uses title **statistics?** It uses statistics because test case execution time is random and what can be better tool than statistics to weed out randomness?

Of course, Author is **yet to apply** this methodology to real life **Industrial scale project** to quantify the benefits of this approach.

To **summarise**, this chapter tells how Mathematics and Statistics can help software professional in general. We took two case studies.

- Application of Mathematics and Statistics for Machine Learning
- Application of Mathematics and Statistics for software projects in general with Authors paper as a case study.

References

1. NCERT Text Books for Mathematics for class 11 and 12, published in India
2. Engineering Mathematics by Croft, Davison, Hargreaves and Flint
3. Bird's Comprehensive Engineering Mathematics, John Bird
4. Introduction to Probability and Statistics for Engineers and Scientists by Sheldon M. Ross
5. Mathematics for Machine Learning Videos by Prof. David Dye and Dr. Sam Cooper both from Imperial College of London
6. Mathematics for Machine Learning by Desisenroth , Failsal and Ong
7. Mathematics of Machine Learning Lecture by Philippe and Machine Learning Math Essentials Lecture Notes by Jeff Howbert
8. The Hundred Page Machine Learning by Burkov
9. Introduction to Machine Learning by Alex Smola and Vishwanathan
10. "Regression Test Suite Execution Time Analysis using Statistical Techniques", International Journal of Education and Management Engineering(IJEME), Vol.6, No.3, pp.33–41, 2016.DOI: 10.5815/ijeme.2016.03.04 by Abhinandan H. Patil

In general without confining to Mathematics for Machine Learning if one wants to learn Mathematics, following are the **great resources.**

Great resources for Mathematics:

1. Anthony Croft, Robert Davison, Martin Hargreaves & James Flint Engineering Mathematics. A Foundation for Electronic, Electrical, Communications and Systems Engineers
2. John Bird Bird's Comprehensive Engineering Mathematics
3. Andrei D. Polyanin & Alexander V. Manzhirov Handbook of Mathematics for Engineers and Scientists
4. Dennis G. Zill & Michael Student Solutions Manual to Accompany Advanced Engineering Mathematics
5. Dennis G. Zill Advanced Engineering Mathematics
6. Erwin kreyszig, Herbert kreyszig & Edward j. norminton Advanced engineering mathematics
7. Hiroyuki Shima, Tsuneyoshi Nakayama Higher Mathematics for Physics and Engineering
8. Dean G. Duffy Advanced Engineering Mathematics

Predicting tech shift in coming years is always difficult; **Here is my Big 5.**

- Renewable Energy
- Digital Transformative Technologies
- Cooling Technology
- Private investment in Aerospace Sectors
- Private Investment in Defense Sectors

All these sectors are STEM dependent. M as in Mathematics.

Some great resources for Probability and Statistics.

1. Methods of Mathematics applied to calculus, probability and statistics by Richard W. Hamming
2. Applied statistics and probability for Engineers Douglas and George

3. Elements of Probability and statistics Francesca and Massimo
4. Probability and statistics for Engineers and Scientists by Sheldon Ross
5. All of statistics: A concise course in statistical interference by Larry
6. Probability and statistics for computer Scientists by Michael Baron
7. Probability and statistics by Heather and Ernest
8. Probability and statistics by Example Yurishov and Mark
9. An Introduction to probability and statistics Vijay Md. Ehsanes
10. Probability Thoery a First course in Probability Theory and statistics Werner Linde
11. Probability and statistics Murray, John and Srinivasan

3

Computer Systems

This chapter is based on single reference[1].

T he chapter is organised into sections as in reference book. Additional reference can be found in [2]

Signals and Number Systems

There are two types of signals in Electronic systems. One that take discrete values and the ones that take continuous values. Former is digital signal and latter is analog signal. Digital representation is more accurate, easy to store and less affected by noise. Analog signals are periodic or non-periodic depending upon whether they repeat after period in time. Example: Sine and Cosine waves are periodic in time. Periodic signals are characterised by Amplitude and frequency. Modern computers store and process information in Digital form. There are two values. Logic "1" and Logic "0" characterised by two voltage levels. Numbers can be represented in various bases. The one that we use for commercial transactions between humans is decimal or base ten. When we say the price of item X is 476 $, we mean, $4*10^2 +7*10^1+6$. There are other number systems such as binary, octal and hexadecimal depending upon the base system chosen.

$$\underbrace{(a_5a_4a_3a_2a_1a_0}_{\text{Integer}} \underbrace{.a_{-1}a_{-2}a_{-3}}_{\text{Fraction}})_r = a_0 \times r^0 + a_1 \times r^1 + a_2 \times r^2 + a_3 \times r^3 + \ldots$$

$$+a_{-1} \times r^{-1} + a_{-2} \times r^{-2} + a_{-2} \times r^{-3} \ldots$$

Number conversion from base r system to decimal

For example to convert binary number $(1111)_2$ to decimal system we just do $1*2^3+1*2^2+1*2^1+1*2^0$ i.e 15. Now let us see how we convert 35 to binary. Since the target number system is smaller than the represented number system,

1. First divide 35 by 2. We get quotient 17 and remainder 1
2. Divide 17 by 2. We get quotient 8 and remainder 1
3. Divide 8 by 2. We get quotient 4 and remainder 0
4. Divide 4 by 2. We get quotient 2 and remainder 0
5. Divide 2 by 2. We get quotient 1 and remainder 0
6. Divide 1 by 2. We get quotient 0 and remainder 1

We arrange the remainders in order 100011. This is binary representation of 35. Now let us arrange 100011 into groups of four bits. i.e (10)(0011) i.e 23_{16}. This shows how we can convert numbers from one system into another. If we have to convert $(3D6)_{16}$ to binary, we convert each hex digit into 4 binary bits. i.e 0011, 1101 and 0110. There fore, $3D6_{16}$ is 001111010110 binary

Complement of binary number is it bits flipped. There fore 0110 complement is 1001. And twos complement is complement + 1. There fore 1001+1 i.e 1010 is twos complement of 0110.

When sign bit is present the MSB (Most significant bit) is sign bit. Thus 13 or $(1101)_2$

is −5 if it is represented in signed number system.

1bit	8 bits	23 bits
S	Biased Exponent	Normalized Mantissa

Biased Exponent and Mantissa in single Precision Representation

Following is table for Binary Coded Decimal

Decimal	BCD
0	0000
1	0001
2	0010
3	0011
4	0100
5	0101
6	0110
7	0111
8	1000
9	1001

BCD Table

Boolean Logic

AND LOGIC: A AND B is 1 iff (if and only if) A is 1 and B is 1. In all other cases it is 0.

OR LOGIC: A OR B is 1 if either A or B is 1.

NOT LOGIC: We just flip the number. Thus NOT 0 is 1 and NOT 1 is 0

NAND LOGIC: is NOT of AND

NOR LOGIC: is NOT of OR

XOR LOGIC: A XOR B is 1 iff (if and only if) only one A or B is 1.
From the Truth table prove that X(Y+Z) = XY+XZ

X	Y	Z	(Y+Z)	XY	XZ	xy+xz	X(Y+Z)
0	0	0	0	0	0	0	0
0	0	1	1	0	0	0	0
0	1	0	1	0	0	0	0
0	1	1	1	0	0	0	0
1	0	0	0	0	0	0	0
1	0	1	1	0	1	1	1
1	1	0	1	1	0	1	1
1	1	1	1	1	1	1	1

Truth Table to prove that X(Y+Z) is same as XY+XZ

Similarly De Morgan's principle which states that (X+Y)' = X' + Y' can be proved

Example Find the complement of F(X+Y+Z) = (X'+Y')(Y+Z')

Taking complement on both the sides,

F'(X+Y+Z)= [(X'+Y')(Y+Z')]'

= (X'+Y')' + (Y+Z')' -> De Morgans principle

= ((XY)')' + ((Y'Z)')' -> De Morgans principle applied to both the brackets

= (XY) + (Y'Z) -> Complement of complement gets cancelled.

Minterm, Maxterm, Karnaugh Map or K-Map and Universal gates

Example:

If function F(X,Y,Z) = XY'Z'+X'YZ'+X'Y'Z then,

each of the terms viz. XY'Z', X'YZ' and X'Y'Z are called **minterms**

Similarly:

If F(X,Y,Z) = (X+Y+Z)(X'+Y'+Z)(X'+Y+Z') then

each of the terms viz. (X+Y+Z), (X'+Y'+Z) and (X'+Y+Z') are called **maxterms**

Example:

Let us look at yet another function

F(X,Y,Z) =XY'Z'+XY'Z+XYZ

using Karnaugh Map

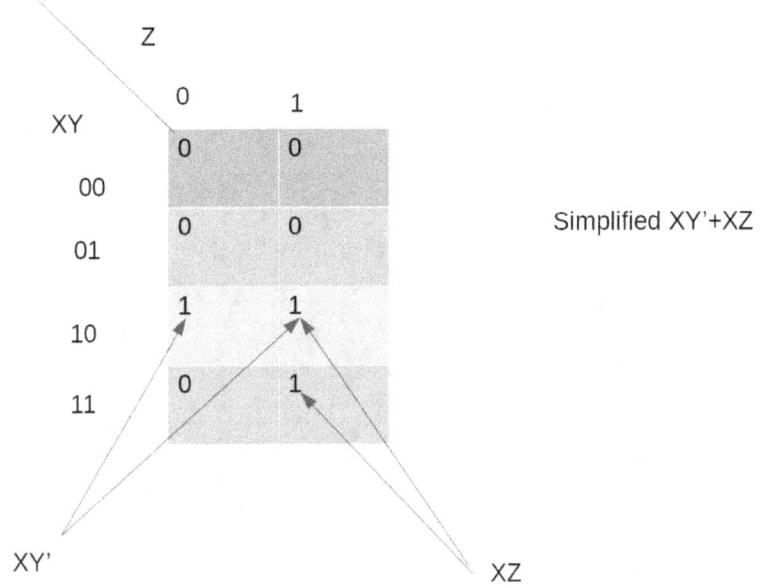

Simplified XY'+XZ

K MAP for the expression XY'Z'+XY'Z+XYZ

X	Y	Z	XY'Z'	XY'Z	XYZ	XY'Z'+XY'Z+XYZ	XZ+XY'
0	0	0	0	0	0	0	0
0	0	1	0	0	0	0	0
0	1	0	0	0	0	0	0
0	1	1	0	0	0	0	0
1	0	0	1	0	0	1	1
1	0	1	0	1	0	1	1
1	1	0	0	0	0	0	0
1	1	1	0	0	1	1	1

Proof that K MAP is correct from Truth Table

Computer Architecture

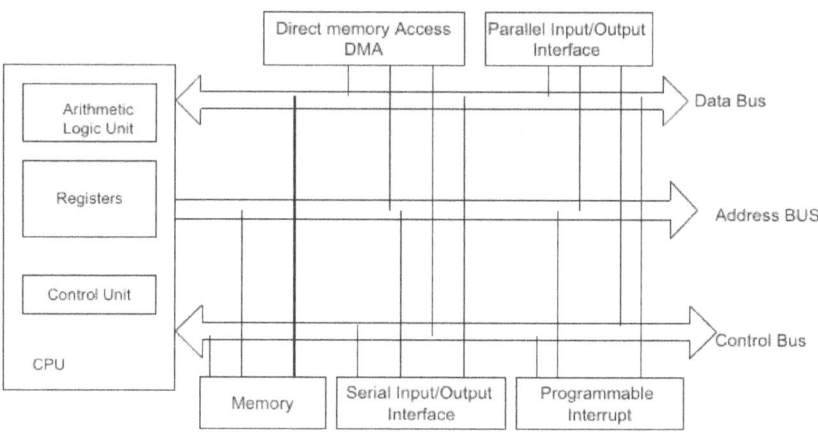

Micro Computer Components

There are two types of Technology RISC (Reduced Instruction Set Computer) and CISC (Complex Instruction Set Computer). CISC consists of large number of instruction set and X86 are examples of CISC. While, RISC consists of limited instruction set. PowerPC, MIPS processor, IBM RISC System/6000, ARM, and SPARC are examples of RISC. Following picture gives conversion from High level language to machine level language

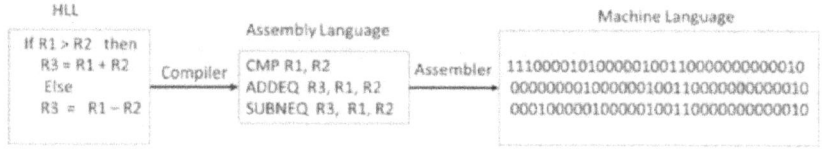

High level language to Machine Level Language

Most of the ARM instructions fall into following category:

(A) Data processing instructions

(B) Single data swap

(C) Shift and rotate instructions

(D) Unconditional instructions and conditional instructions

(E) Stack operations

(F) Branch

(G) Multiply instructions

(H) Data transfer

More about the Assembly language programming is covered in the subsequent chapters.

REFERENCES

1. Computer Systems by Ata Elahi, Springer publications.
2. The Architecture of Computer hardware, system software and Networking by Irv Englander

4

Software Quality Assurance

Why Software Quality Assurance aka Software Testing is third chapter in this Book? Soon you will know. But for the time being Software Testing is as essential as development.

One thing that has not changed in the last 25 years is the fact that software testing is lion share of total budget of software life cycle. If we have to quantify it, its is 50+%. In academic circles, software testing was small chapter in software engineering books. Today you see books and dedicated post graduate courses being offered in software testing. A look at the number of books in Reference section or search on search engines for postgraduate courses should justify this fact.

In this chapter we shall touch upon theory and practices that lead to production grade software. We shall also talk about requirements, defects, test cases, test results, verification of software against requirements and validation of software against test oracles etc. Then we shall move on to Unit, Integration, System and Acceptance testing.

Software Quality, rather difficult term to define is an intangible attribute of software which decides the success or failure of the product/organisation in general is mainly decided by the effectiveness of software testing and process followed in the project or organisation. Software Quality revolution started in Japan/USA simultaneously. The earliest documents date back to as early as 1950. The earliest documents are Shewart's cycle which talks about PDCA

(Short for Plan, Do, Check and Act) and Ishikawa diagram which is essentially { {Materials, Methods}, {Machines, Measurements}} -> Quality. Where { } means combined and -> means leads to.

Software testing can be

· Static as in code inspection and code review
· Dynamic as in Actual execution to expose failure

The other thing that is talked much about is Fault -> Error -> Failure or Fault leads to Failure in short. Example developer trying to divide number by 0 or trying to access the memory out of bounds in C programming language are Faults and the resulting core dump is example of Failure.

Another important attribute of software is reliability. We often hear about telecom networking companies talking about 99.9999% up time which is essentially reliability of the software. The main objective of the testing is to catch the bugs and catch them early, to reduce risk and reduce cost of testing.

What is Test Case?

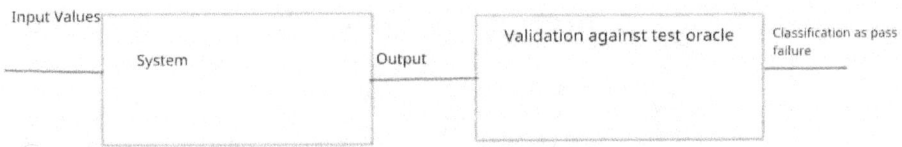

Test Case Illustrated

As shown in the diagram above, test case consists of input values or test data and system accepts this input and produces output which then is validated against the test oracle to classify the execution of test case as pass or failure.

Two popular software models are V and Agile. We shall take up Agile later. Let us take a look at V model and see which testing phase fits where.

V Model:

· Acceptance test cases are designed at the same time as Requirements.

- System test cases are written at the same as product high level design
- Integration test cases are written at the same time as low level design
- Unit test cases are written at the same time as coding by developers

Yet another term we often hear about testing is Regression testing. Regression testing is the activity which is carried out to ensure that any new functionality introduced does not break existing code or existing functionality. Or in other words with new functionality system should not regress. Regression testing can be at Unit, Integration or System testing level.

Next is how do we design the test cases?. Test cases are ideally designed on the basis of requirement specifications. Other sources could be code (White box approach) or the basis of input-output domain(Black box). Planning, Design, Monitoring and Measurement are the important phases of testing.

What are test tools? Anything and everything that leads to increased test productivity of tester, leads to better coverage, results in reduction of duration test phases, leads to increased effectiveness can be classified as test Tool.

Now let us touch upon some of the industry specific certifications:

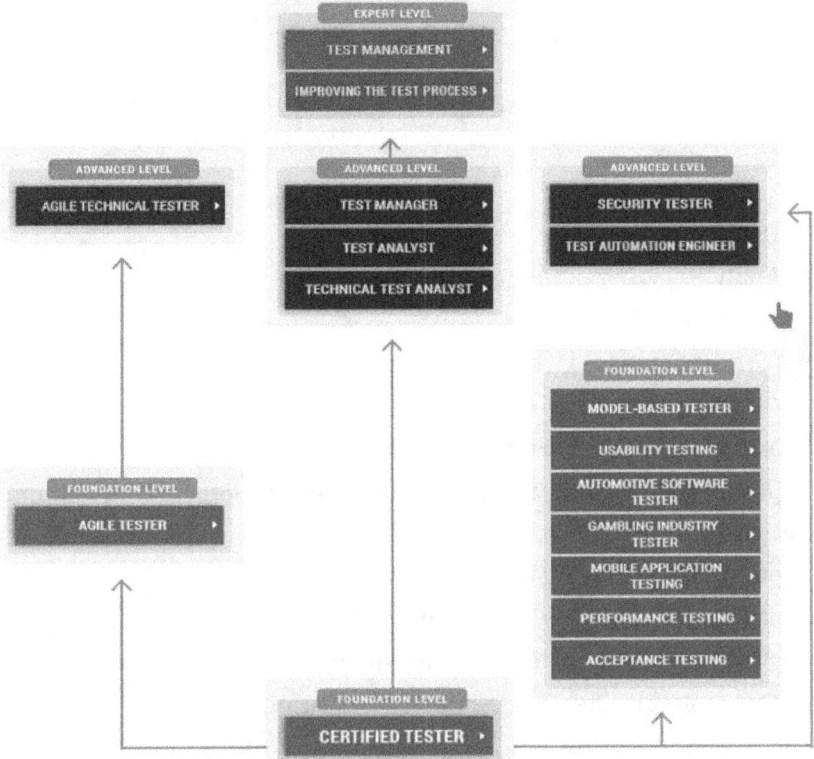

ISTQB Certification Portfolio

In this book we will be covering core track:

- Certified Tester Foundation Level
- Test Analyst
- Test Manager

We will be touching upon Agile track with:

- Agile Tester Foundations

3.1 Certified Tester Foundation Level

The certification tests testers on three parameters

- K1: Remeber
- K2: Understand
- K3: Apply

Syllabus for the same is

- Chapter 1: 175 minutes Fundamentals of Testing
- Chapter 2: 100 minutes Testing Throughout the Software Development Lifecycle
- Chapter 3: 135 minutes Static Testing
- Chapter 4: 330 minutes Test Techniques
- Chapter 5: 225 minutes Test Management
- Chapter 6: 40 minutes Tool Support for Testing

Now let us see what they cover.

3.1.1 Fundamentals of Testing

- Necessity of testing: Humans and others are causes of software defects. Human actions result in error. Error leads to Defect or bug. Defect leads to failure. This is already mentioned.
- Role of testing on product quality: The effective testing and product quality are related.
- Exhaustive testing will never be a possibility. Testing has to be concluded at some logical point
- Testing consists of following activities:

1. Test planning: This is the activity during which scope, approach, resources and schedule are established.

2. Test control: Any deviation from test plan is corrected in this activity
3. Test Analysis: Identify what to test
4. Test Design: Activity to determine how to test what is decided to be tested. Activity where test plan is translated into tangible test cases
5. Test implementation: Developing and prioritising test procedures, test data and setting up test environment.
6. Test execution: Actual test execution.
7. Checking results: Checking results and outcome of test execution
8. Evaluating the exit criteria: Where quality needs are balanced against other project priorities and constraints.
9. Test results reporting: Reporting test progress against exit criteria
10. Test closure: This is when closure is done with relevant test metrics and re-usable test wares etc.

• Seven Testing principles

1. Principle 1: Testing process shows the presence of defects and it cannot prove the absence of defects.
2. Principle 2: Exhaustive testing is impossible.
3. Principle 3: Start the testing early
4. Principle 4: Defects tend to be clustered
5. Principle 5: Pesticide paradox: Same testing repeated over and again will no longer find the new defects.
6. Principle 6: Testing is context sensitive meaning testing for health care and safety critical testing will not be the same
7. Principle 7: Absence of errors fallacy: If the software is error free but unusable and if it does not meet users expectations it is zero sum.

• Attributes of tester and Code of Ethics. Following are the traits of testers

1. Curiosity
2. Critical eye
3. Detail oriented

4. Experience
5. Good communication

In addition to these testers must possess highest level of ethics.

3.1.2 Testing throughout the software life cycle

According to the accepted prevailing knowledge, testing at the end of life cycle as in case of water fall model is inadequate. There fore the models that employ testing throughout the life cycle are employed. One such model is V model which is already discussed. Next let us look at the Iterative life cycles.Examples of Iterative life cycle models are:

- Rapid Application Development: This is parallel development of functions and subsequent integration. And in each function development, Define, Develop, Build and Test is followed.
- Agile Development: There are two important things to discuss in Agile development i.e (a) Agile software development and (b) Agile manifesto. let us discuss both of them

1. Agile is iterative and incremental where requirements evolve
2. Agile manifesto: This tells what is valued in this way of working.

(i) Individual and interactions over processes and tools
  (ii) Working software over comprehensive documentation
  (iii) Customer collaboration over contract negotiation
  (iv) Responding to change over following plan

- Test levels:

1. Component testing. Also called Unit testing or module testing Makes use of stub and drivers. Stub is called component and driver is calling component.

2. Integration testing. Testing designed to expose defects in component interaction or component interfaces.
3. System testing. Behaviour of the whole system or product is tested.
4. Acceptance testing. It is a formal testing with respect to user needs and requirements.

· Testing types:

1. Functional testing: Cross checking the functionality of component or system against specifications
2. Non functional testing: Testing reliability, usability, efficiency, main-tainability, security and portability
3. Structural testing: Measuring the thoroughness with respect to coverage items. Code coverage is an example of structural testing with respect to code.
4. Conformation testing and Regression testing

3.1.3 Static testing techniques:

Static testing is a testing where component or system is tested without execution. It is opposite of dynamic testing where actual execution of component or system is done.

· Review process:

1. Review process consists of Planning, kick-off, preparation, review meeting, rework and follow-up.
2. Moderator, Author, reviewer and manager are roles of review process
3. Walk through and inspection are types of review

· Static Analysis by Tools

1. Process of checking the code for adherence to coding standards

2. Checking code metrics with respect to cyclomatic complexity etc.
3. Checking control flow structure, data flow structure and data structures etc.

3.1.4 Test design techniques

In Test design we encounter important term called test case specification where test cases are specified with respect to objective, inputs, expected results and execution preconditions. Another important term is traceability which maps the items in documents to software item.

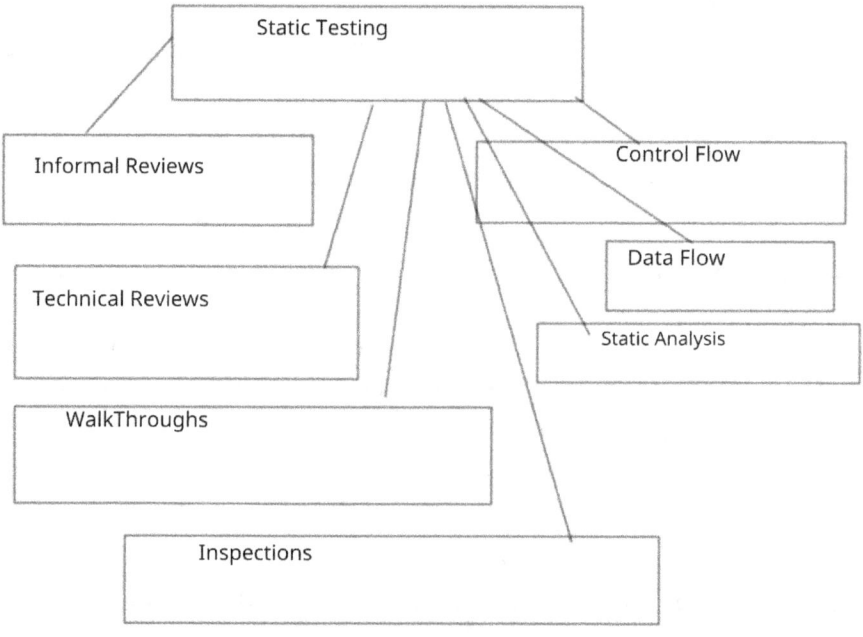

Static testing techniques

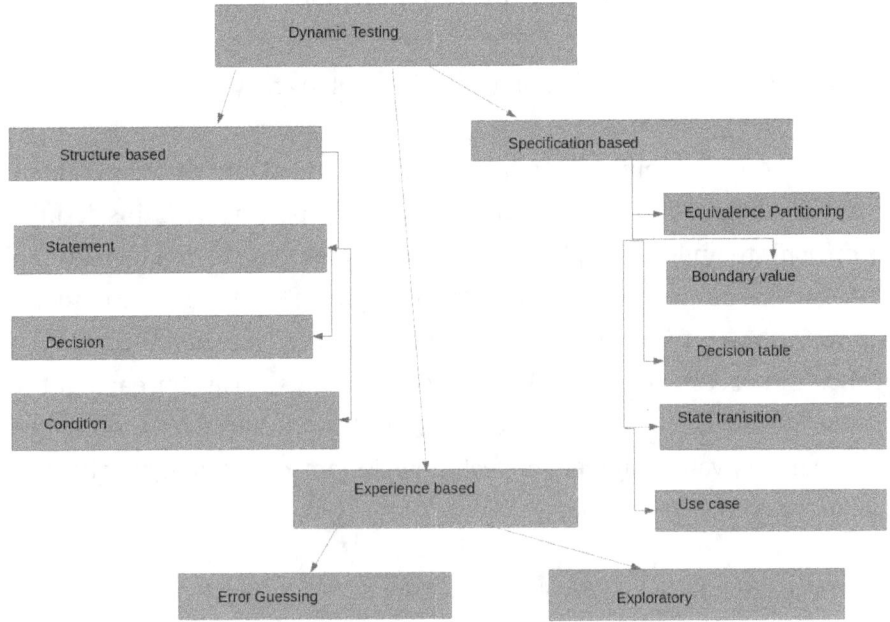

Dynamic Testing Techniques

Test development process would consist of

- Test Analysis where test conditions are analysed
- Test design
- Test implementation

Following are categories of test design tecchniques

- Static testing: Where no test cases are executed and generally done before test cases are executed on software
- Specification based, black box
- Structure based, white box
- Experience based

Now let us look at each one of them in detail.

Specification based or black box testing techniques

· Equivalence partitioning and boundary value analysis:

In this approach input or output domain are divided into partitions and test cases are designed to represent the each of these partitions. If this definition is difficult to understand, let us take a concrete example. Let us take banks interest rate as an example. Let us say bank pays 3% interest rate for deposit up to $100, 5% for deposit greater than $100 but less than $1000, 7% for deposit in excess of $1000. We have to design test cases for each of these cases. We may also want to test for $99.9, $100.1, $999.9, $1000.1. These are boundary values and testing technique is named accordingly as boundary value analysis

· Decision table based testing

Let us take credit card with following discount policy

1. New customer gets 15% discount
2. Existing customer with loyalty card gets 10% discount
3. If the customer has coupon 20% discount

Discount amounts are added if applicable

New customer (15%)	Loyalty card (10%)	Coupon (20%)	Discount(%)
T	T	T	Not possible
T	T	F	Not possible
T	F	F	20%
T	F	T	15%
F	T	T	30%
F	T	F	10%
F	F	T	20%
F	F	F	0

Decision Table for Credit Card Example

Now test cases need to be added for each of the cases of Decision table

- State transition diagram based testing

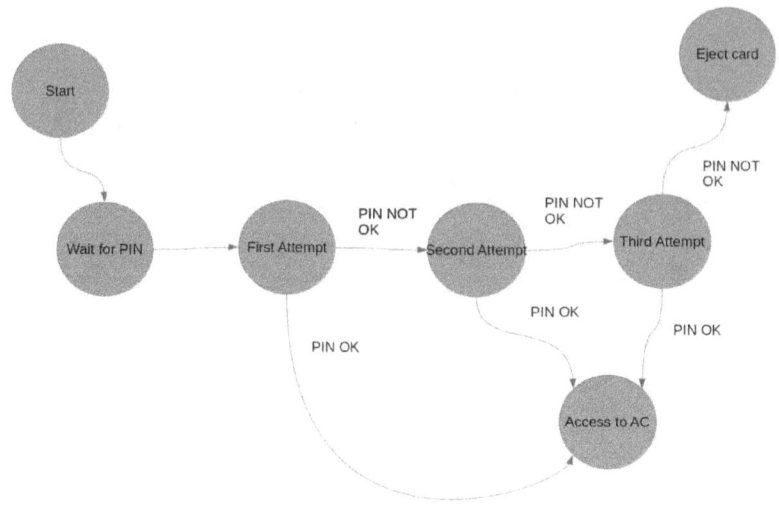

State transition for PIN entry

State transition testing is black box approach where valid and invalid state transitions are tested with unique test cases. State transition diagram shows the various states of component or system and events that cause the state transition. Telecom system software comprises some of the most complex state transition diagrams.

- Use case based testing

Use case based testing is a black box approach where test cases are designed to execute scenarios of use cases.

- Structure or white box based testing

Is as mentioned in the head lines is white box based testing approach. It is coverage based where coverage is defined as follows:

Coverage = Number of coverage items exercised/Total number of coverage items

1. Statement coverage: Statement coverage= Number of statements exercised/Total number of statements.
2. Decision coverage: Decision coverage= Number of decision outcomes exercised/Total number of Decisions.
3. Branch coverage: Branch coverage= Number of branches exercised/Total number of Branches

- Experience based testing technique

1. Error guessing
2. Exploratory testing : An informal approach where tester uses the information and knowledge gained while testing to further improve the test design and test cases

- Choosing test technique

There is test technique which fits all the needs all the time. Each test technique has its own advantages and benefits. Combination of test techniques can be used depending upon the need of testing.

3.1.5 Test management

Test management involves planning, estimating, monitoring and control of test activities. Test Manager(Test Leader) is the one who is at the helm of these activities. Let us look at the each components one by one.

- Test Planning

This is the first step of test management. Let us look at how the test plan document looks like:

Test Plan according to IEEE 829-1998

1. Test plan identifier
2. Introduction
3. Test items
4. Features to be tested
5. Features not to be tested
6. Approach
7. Item pass/fail criteria (test exit criteria)
8. Suspension criteria and resumption requirements
9. Test deliverables
10. Testing tasks
11. Environmental needs
12. Responsibilities
13. Staffing and training needs
14. Schedule
15. Risk and contingencies
16. Approvals

IEEE 829 Test Plan Template

The IEEE 829-1998 template is self explanatory and explains test plan documents outline.

- Test Estimation

This process is estimating what testing will involve and how much it will cost.

- Test Monitoring and Control

This activity involves monitoring and control. Test logs and test reports aid this activity

---

IEEE 829 STANDARD: TEST LOG TEMPLATE

Test log identifier
Description (items being tested,
environment in which the testing is
conducted)

Activity and event entries (execution
description, procedure results,
environmental information,
anomalous events, incident report
identifiers)

IEEE 829 Test Log Template

IEEE 829 STANDARD:
TEST SUMMARY REPORT TEMPLATE

Test summary report identifier
Summary
Variances
Comprehensive assessment
Summary of results

Evaluation
Summary of activities
Approvals

IEEE 829 Test Summary Report

Yet another term that we encounter is incident management.

Incident management is the process of recognising, investigating, taking actions and closing the incidents. Typical incident report cycle involves

Reported -> Opened ->Assigned -> Fixed -> Closed. However the incident could be Rejected, Deferred or Reopened in few cases.

3.1.6 Tools support for testing

The benefits of using Test tools involves reduction of repetitive work. It means consistency, repeatability, objective assessment.

Classification on the basis of support for testing and tests	Test Management Tools
	Requirement Management Tools
	Incident Management Tools
	Configuration Management Tools
Static testing Tools	Review Tools
	Statuc analysis Tools
	Modeling Tools
Test specification Tools	Test design Tools
	Test data preparation Tools
Test execution and Logging	Test execution Tools
	Test harness/unit test frame works
	Test comparators
	Coverage measurement Tools
	Security testing Tools
Tools support for performance and monitoring	Dynamic analysis Tools
	Performance testing, load and stress testing Tools
	Monitoring Tools

Test Tool Classification

3.2 Certified Test Analyst

This certification tests over and above what is tested in foundation level. The course syllabus by certifying authority for example below gives the idea of what is expected.

Chapter 1: The Technical Test Analyst's Tasks in Risk-Based Testing
- Risk identification
- Risk assessment
- Risk mitigation

Chapter 2: White-Box Test Techniques
- White-Box test techniques
- Selecting a white-box test technique

Chapter 3: Analytical Techniques
- Static analysis
- Dynamic analysis

Chapter 4: Quality Characteristics for Technical Testing
- General planning issues
- Security testing
- Reliability testing
- Performance efficiency testing
- Maintainability testing
- Portability testing
- Compatibility testing

Chapter 5: Reviews
- Using checklists in reviews
- Architectural reviews
- Code Reviews

Chapter 6: Test Tools & Automation
- Defining the test automation project
- Specific test tools

ISTQB Test Analysts Syllabus

3.3 Certified Test Manager

This certification is for test managers.

3.4 Agile Testing

Two important items in this are Agile manifesto and Agile Principles. Let us look at them

- Individuals and interactions *over* processes and tools
- Working software *over* comprehensive documentation
- Customer collaboration *over* contract negotiation
- Responding to change *over* following a plan

Agile Manifesto

Principles

The core Agile Manifesto values are captured in twelve principles:

- Our highest priority is to satisfy the customer through early and continuous delivery of valuable software.
- Welcome changing requirements, even late in development. Agile processes harness change for the customer's competitive advantage.
- Deliver working software frequently, at intervals of between a few weeks to a few months, with a preference to the shorter timescale.
- Business people and developers must work together daily throughout the project.
- Build projects around motivated individuals. Give them the environment and support they need, and trust them to get the job done.
- The most efficient and effective method of conveying information to and within a development team is face-to-face conversation.
- Working software is the primary measure of progress.
- Agile processes promote sustainable development. The sponsors, developers, and users should be able to maintain a constant pace indefinitely.
- Continuous attention to technical excellence and good design enhances agility.
- Simplicity—the art of maximizing the amount of work not done—is essential.
- The best architectures, requirements, and designs emerge from self-organizing teams.
- At regular intervals, the team reflects on how to become more effective, then tunes and adjusts its behavior accordingly.

Agile principles

REFERENCES

1. Bath, Graham, and Erik van Veenendaal. *Improving the Test Process: Implementing Improvement and Change—a Study Guide for the ISTQB Expert Level Module.* 1st edition, Rocky Nook Inc, 2014.

2. Berk, Joseph, and Susan Berk. *Quality Management for the Technology Sector.* Newnes, 2000.

3. Black, Rex, et al. *Agile Testing Foundations: An ISTQB Foundation Level Agile Tester Guide.* 2017.

4. Black, Rex, and Jamie L. Mitchell. *Advanced Software Testing*. 1st ed, Rocky Nook, 2009.

5. Dick, Scott, and Abraham Kandel. *Computational Intelligence in Software Quality Assurance*. World Scientific, 2005.

6. *FOUNDATIONS OF SOFTWARE TESTING ISTQB CERTIFICATION, 4TH EDITION*. CENGAGE LEARNING EMEA, 2019.

7. Naik, Kshirasagar, and Priyadarshi Tripathy. *Software Testing and Quality Assurance: Theory and Practice*. John Wiley & Sons, 2008.

8. Roman, Adam. *The ISTQB Foundation Level 2018 Syllabus: Test Techniques and Sample Exams*. 1st edition, Springer Berlin Heidelberg, 2018.

9. Tian, Jeff. *Software Quality Engineering: Testing, Quality Assurance, and Quantifiable Improvement*. John Wiley & Sons, Inc., 2005. *DOI.org (Crossref)*, doi:10.1002/0471722324.

5

Scripting

S cripting has its own place in Software Engineering. Batch processing of commands to achieve meaningful tasks is achieved using scripting. Python or Perl can be used for scripting. However, the following Authoritative documents are for Shell Scripting

1. Linux Command Line and Shell Scripting Bible by Richard and Christine
2. Shell Scripting by Steve Parker
3. Linux Shell Scripting with Bash by Ken O. Burtch
4. Mastering Linux Shell Scripting by Andrew.

6

Choice of Operating Systems for Software Development

Although the Author of this Book wanted to discuss this topic. It appears that it is a solved problem. Answer is Linux for servers and Windows/Mac for Desktops. If you are a developer looking for development environment for most of the cases Linux+Debian+Ubuntu or Mac should be the OS. For Desktop Windows/Mac ace. However Linux can also be used for Desktop.

7

Traditional Programming Languages such as Assembly, C, C++

T his chapter will be broadly classified into following categories

1. Assembly language programming
2. C Programming
3. C++ Programming

Why one needs to learn multiple programming language? The answer is simple. There is no "One size fits all" solution available as far as programming languages. For specific purpose the desired programming language needs to be learned. Choice of the programming language is primary responsibility of Chief Architect of the project. The choice is arrived at after much deliberation and quantifiable data of prototypes. We are avoiding getting into those details.

4.1 Assembly language programming

Performance critical programming code snippets tend to be written in assembly language and they are called from external C/C++ code. Generally for higher level compiled languages, the sequence is compilation followed by linking followed by executable. For assembly level languages the assemblers does the same job. We have assemblers like

1) Microsoft Macro Assembler (MASM)

2) Netwide Assembler (NASM)

MASM is popular for Microsoft platforms while NASM is popular for Linux platforms.

Let us look at the processor architecture

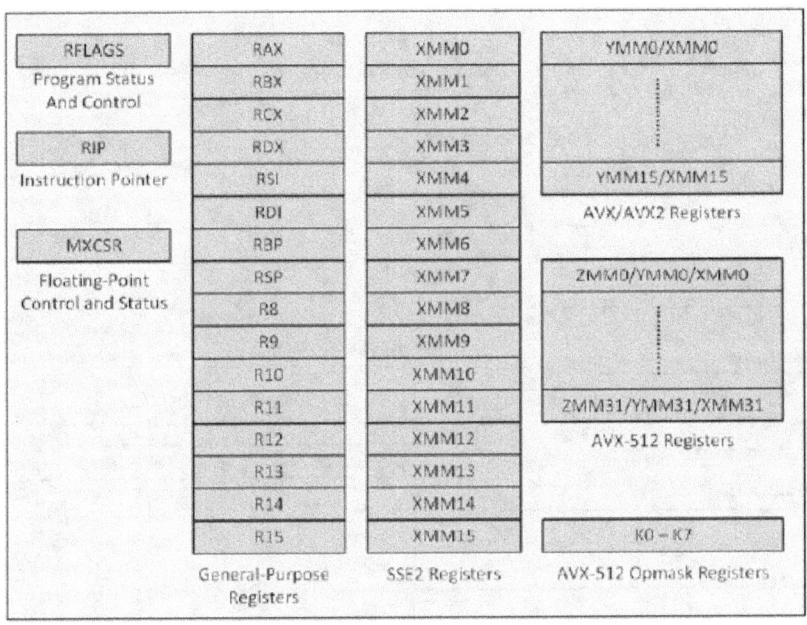

X86-64 Processor Architecture Logical View 1

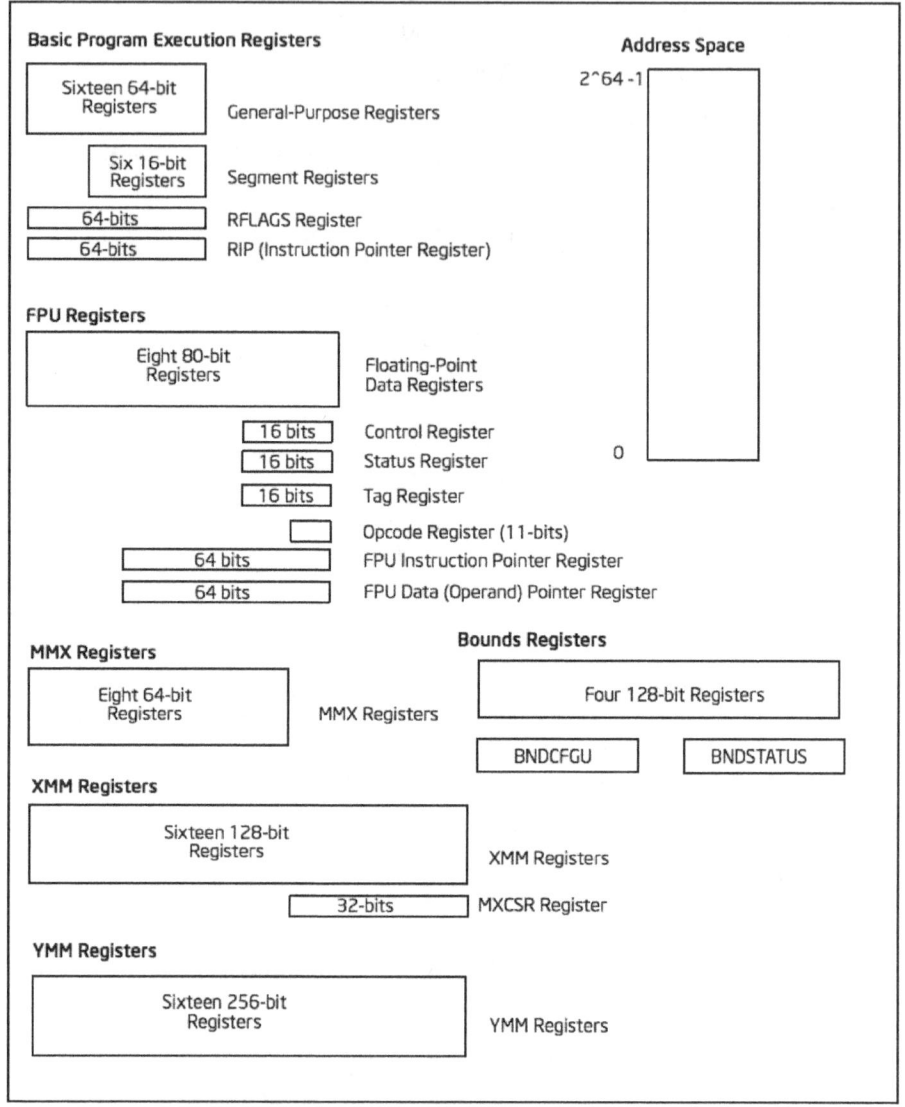

X86–64 Processor Architecture Logical View 2

As you can see there are limited number of registers with which you need code. The code will consist of series of instructions. Instructions are combination of mnemonics and operands. There are three addressing modes.

1) Immediate where one of the operand is number

2) Register where both the operands are registers

3) Memory where one of the operands is memory location

Now let us look at the assembly level language code snippet.

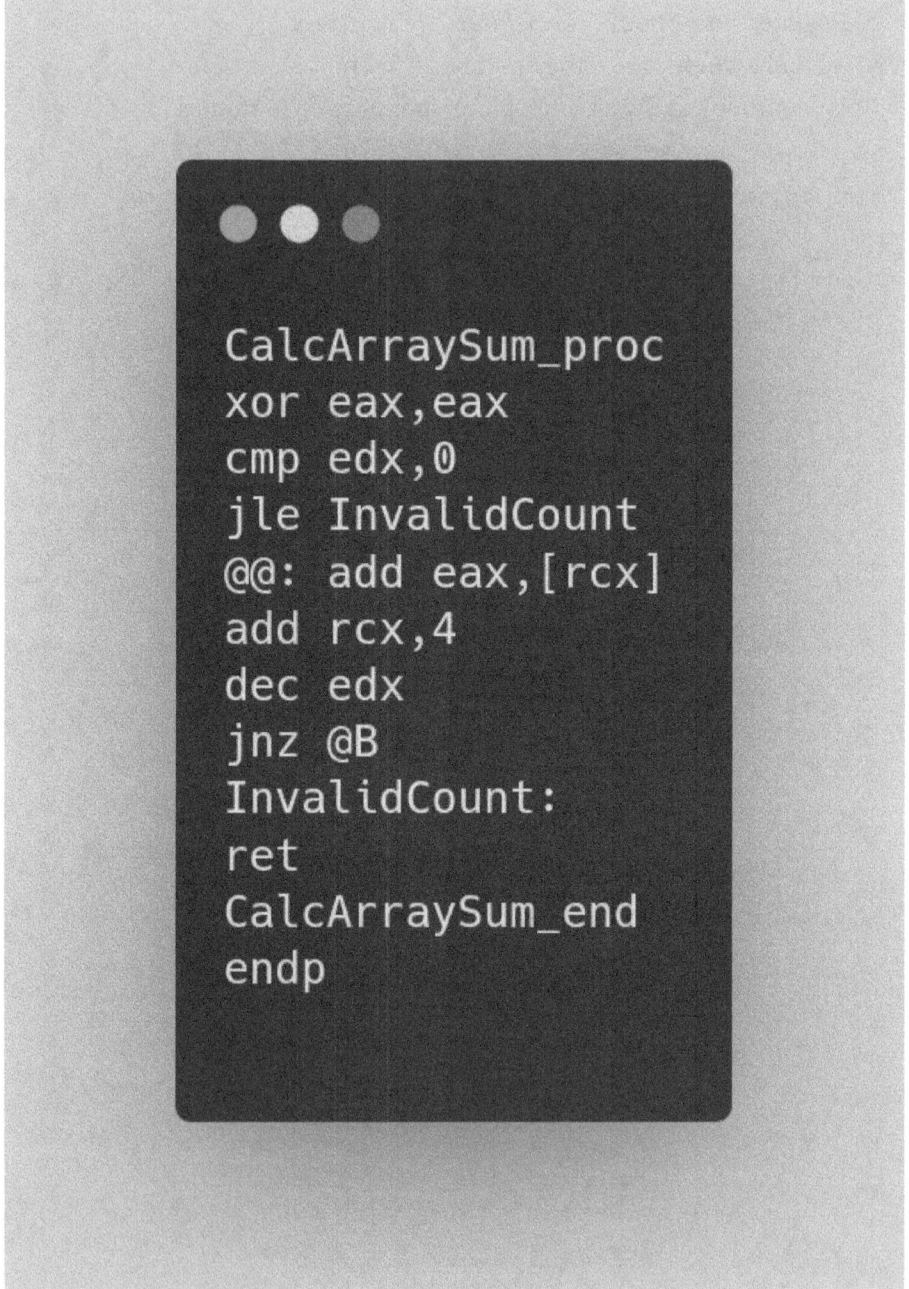

```
CalcArraySum_proc
xor eax,eax
cmp edx,0
jle InvalidCount
@@: add eax,[rcx]
add rcx,4
dec edx
jnz @B
InvalidCount:
ret
CalcArraySum_end
endp
```

Assembly Language Code Snippet for Calculating the Sum of Array

This code snippet needs bit of explanation. First eax is supposed to hold the final sum. It is initialised to zero by xoring with self. You know xor of a number with self is zero. edx holds the count of entities in the array. First we check if it is less than or equal to zero. If it is we do not enter the loop. If it is greater than zero, we enter the loop. To begin with rcx holds the base address of the array. We go on incrementing the address with size of the number which in this case is 4 byte. We decrement the loop count simultaneously. When the loop count becomes zero, we return.

The intention of this whole exercise was to show that for simple array element addition, the code becomes unreadable. We are living in times when the application code hits million lines easily. Imagine maintaining assembly code with poor or no comments. That is the reason companies using assembly languages are far and few. Even those who are using assembly languages, they are coding only performance critical blocks in assembly language and then calling them from C/C++.

There are stories about companies going bust because of ill commented assembly language codes. Let us move on!!

4.2 C Programming Language

C was default programming language for system programmers for long time. It is closest to assembly language when it comes to performance at the same time offers all the benefits of intermediate programming language. In the early nineties this was one of the most used and sought after programming language. C is basically used for following reasons

- Ease of learning
- Portability
- Efficiency
- Hardware interfacing capabilities
- It is foundation programming language
- Legacy projects

Let us learn each of these points. C is easy to learn as it is minimalist. Just contains what is required. Source code is portable. Meaning as long as you have target {compiler, linker and loaders} (Which these days are part of one tool example gcc), the source code is portable. Programs are efficient as they are fast. C is one of the best languages for hardware interfacing. Last but not least, many open source and commercial projects are still in C programming language. Although open source programming languages like GO are more relevant these days, you may have to learn or revisit the C programming language just like Fortran. For example open source scientific tool Octave still has some of the code base in Fortran.

Now what do we mean by Foundation ? We mean that many programming languages like Java and Python are them selves written using C.

Like any procedural programming language, you need to know:

- Keywords
- variables and values
- Functions
- Operators
- Enumerations
- Structures (And Unions)
- Derived data types such as Arrays, Linkedlist, Trees, Stacks and Queues etc

4.2.1 Extending C

C programming language has two types of functions namely

- Built in
- Non built in

Built in functions can be invoked by including appropriate header files. There are two types of libraries that you can link you programs with

- Static library mainly *.a
- Dynamic library mainly *.so

What is the difference ? Static library code get embedded in the final executable while shared library code is not embedded and is dynamically linked. Integrated development environments like Code::Blocks are very handy for the development projects of C. Now let us move on to next programming languages.

Pointers in C is most debated topic. Well it can be advantageous or curse depending upon how it is used. While the system architecture protects it self from malicious access nothing prevents programs from accessing its own memory in unintended way leading to crash which is also called core dump. You need debuggers to analyse the core dumps.

Next nothing prevents programs from accessing array index out of bounds or dividing number by zero etc. In addition to these, when ever you allocate memory from heap, { The memory is divided into Code, Data, Heap and Stack } you need to free up the memory after usage. Else it leads to memory leaks which results in performance degradation.

4.3 C++, Object Oriented Programming Language

In theory, C++ is supposed to be super set of C programming language. Meaning C++ supports or has all the features listed in 4.2 but also has additional features. A quick look over the internet shows that there are various C++ compilers. Such as

- g++ which stands for GNU C++ compiler
- Clang an open source C++ compiler for various platforms
- Visual C++ community by Microsoft Corporation

And there are few others.

Now there is standard body which governs the standardisation across the various compilers. In essence it is the minimal number of features that the given compiler should support in addition to having its own features if need be. Let us not get into further details of standardisation. Instead let us look at the language features. In general the programming languages can be

- Procedural programming languages
- Object oriented programming language

C++ falls into latter. However, g++ compiler can be used to compile most of the C programs as well.

- While using the C++ programming language, the designer tries to solve practical word problems by mapping everything into objects.
- Object is Class in action. Generally objects will have data and methods to works on those data
- C++ in theory is super set of C. In theory you can write procedure oriented programs in C++. Although abuse of C++, that is what novice C++ programmers do during the learning curve. In general Object Oriented PL is super set of Procedure Oriented PL which is super set of Assembly level language which is super set of machine level language .
- C++ supports data encapsulation. Meaning, the data is confined to the objects and can be operated upon by methods of the same object. When data type is static all the instances of the objects share same copy of data. On the other hand, static member functions cannot access non static data types.
- In C++ there are three types of access control viz. public, private and protected. When the data type is private, the data type can be only accessed using the member functions of the objects. Only exception is Friend function. When the data type is public they can be accessed using the "." notation. Let us defer the protected till the concept of Inheritance.
- Next is initialisation of objects using Constructors and Destructors. The object constructor is invoked via special public function and with syntax ClassName(Arguments). In the constructor all the data encapsulated by the object is initialised with valid initial values. The object is Destructed

using the syntax **~ClassName( )**. Ensure to free up memory allocated on heap using the Destructors.

- Function overloading. This is feature of C++ where you can use same function name but call different versions of the methods depending upon number or type of the data types.
- Default values of the Arguments to function. In the function signature you can set the default values of the arguments and relieve calling functions from passing the arguments to the function.
- Inline functions ensure that the function code gets embedded in the objects. Although object size may increase, the speed of execution gets boosted. It is trade off between size of the objects vs speed.
- References. Achieved using pointers. Advantage: When method arguments are passed by value, copy of the data types is created on the stack. Instead the function arguments can be passed as reference and return values can also be reference. In this case the stack will have only pointer address.
- Operator overloading is a concept where special meaning is assigned to the standard operators. C++ behaves different with respect to the operator depending upon the context.
- Dynamic object creation and destruction: In C memory is allocated using the malloc and freed using the free. In C++ objects are created using the keyword new and destructed using the delete. Do not forget to have equal number of delete as new. Else you will run into memory leak issues. Memory leak proof code is very essential for programs which tend to run over prolonged period of time. Example: Servers.
- Inheritance is one of the potent features of C++ where you Inherit from the base class and add additional functionality or data or both in the derived class. For example in **class Y : public X** class Y inherits publically from base class X.
- Next is virtual functions. Let us say the inheritance order is Locomotive -> Car -> Ferrari. And let us say some function drive is defined as **virtual** in Locomotive, when you reference object of Ferrari using Locomotive and invoke the drive, the binding is deferred till run time and actual function

of Ferrari gets invoked although pointer is of type Locomotive.

· Templates: The syntax for for template can be like:

```
template<class T>
  class Array {
  ...
  };
  and can be invoked using,
  int main() {
  Array<int> ia;
  Array<float> fa;
  That is code can be reused for different data types.
```

REFRENCES

1. *Assembly Language for X86 Processors.*
2. Learn to Program with C Noel Kalicharan
3. Problem Solving and Program Design in C by Hanley and Kofman
4. Beginning C++17 or C++20 Ivor Horton Peter Van Weert
5. SamsTeachYourself C++ by Siddhartha Rao
6. Clean C++ Stephan Roth
7. Modern C++ for Absolute Beginners Slobodan Dmitrović
8. Object oriented programming in C++ by Robert Lafore
9. The C++ Standard Library Nicolai M. Josuttis
10. Working draft, Standard for C++ programming language, 2017

8

Rust and Golang

It appears that Rust and Golang combined will replace C/C++ in future. Legacy applications will be migrated to modern programming languages such as Rust and Golang for various reasons. Rust is particularly useful for Embedded, Networking and Web . It appears that, Rust and Golang will be used as backend programming languages in Web for their performance reasons. Some of the important reference Books for Rust and Golang include:

1. The Rust Programming Language (Covers Rust 2018) Book by Carol Nichols and Steve Klabnik
2. Rust by example on line book https://doc.rust-lang.org/rust-by-example/
3. Note worthy git repository https://github.com/klemola/rust-book
4. The Go Programming Language Book by Alan A. A. Donovan and Brian Kernighan

9

Java, Scala, Kotlin Programming Language

J ava is still being used as a programming language for enterprise applications. In particular spring frame work and spring boot applications are keeping interest in Java. Scala and Java are still being used for the server side programming. While Kotlin is recommended programming language for Android app development. You could read the following .

1. JDK documentation Approximately 50 MB in size
2. Java for Absolute Beginners by Iuliana Cosmina
3. Java in a Nutshell, Seventh Edition by Ben Evans and David Flanagan
4. Java Program Design Principles, Polymorphism and Patterns by Edward Sciore
5. Modern Java in Action by Raoul-gabriel urma, Mario fusco, and Alan mycroft
6. Functional Programming in Java by Pierre-yves saumont
7. Modern Java Recipes Ken Kousen

10

JavaScript as Programming Language

P erhaps most popular web development language. Frame works such as React, Angular and Vue3 for front end and Express+Node for back end are keeping it as most widely used programming language. Reference material to begin with:

1. To get you going and quick reference: JavaScript Handbook by Flavio Copes (56 pages)
2. Comprehensive Book on JavaScript: JavaScript Novice to Ninja Second Edition by Darren Jones (665 pages)
3. Eloquent JavaScript by Marijn Haverbeke

HTML5 and CSS3 which are Hyper Text Markup Language and Cascaded Style Sheet repetitively used as front end languages for Web programming.

1. Sams Teach Yourself HTML and CSS in 24 Hours
2. Sams TeachYourself HTML, CSS & JavaScript Web Publishing

Plenty of good online courses on Udemy and other portals.

11

Python Programming Language

P ython is probably most widely used programming language because of its rich libraries ranging from Scipy, Sympy for scientific application to Flask, Django for web development to Scikit learn and Keras+Tensorflow for machine learning. Already Python is documented by Authors in the following study material:

1. Python Tutorial Release 3.8.3 by Guido Van Rossum and Python Development team.
2. Beginning Python by Magnus Lie Hetland
3. Think Python by Allen B. Downey
4. Python Essential Reference by David M. Beazley
5. Python Cookbook by David Beazley and Brian K. Jones

Python usage case studies:

1. Learning IPython for Interactive Computing and Data Visualization Book by Cyrille Rossant where Author demonstrates how you can use Python for various purpose
2. Python for Probability, Statistics, and Machine Learning Book by José Unpingco shows how Python can be used for Probability, Statistics and Machine Learning

3. Scipy Lecture Notes
4. Sympy documentation

Many good Python courses in Udemy and other portals.

Following Git Hub repository for Python are working relentlessly to make Python popular

url = https://github.com/vinta/awesome-python

url = https://github.com/realpython/materials.git

12

Visual Programming

Visual Programming is part of No Code and Low Code movement. Visual Programming is one step closer to Human Convenience as you are getting closer to Human from Machine Understandable languages. Plus programming will be used by Citizen developers who need not have computer science or software engineering or programming background. Studies indicate that Low Code/ No Code will be adopted in Big ways by 2025 and Beyond.

Case study:

When Engineers moved from Assembly to C, it was great. It was movement from Machine readable format to Human readable format. One step closer to Human convenience. Then there was an attempt 15-20 years back to take the programming one step further. Auto generate code from Visuals {Ex: Telelogic for Telecom domain, Rational for General purpose etc}. The tools as such had no major issues. The issues if any were either exaggerated or stemmed from lack of knowledge of the Tools themselves. Result? We had to stick to Human Readable **text programming** for so long. Had the Engineering community given Visual Programming Tools opportunity, Tools would have matured in last two decades. As they say One Visual is worth thousand words. May be Visual programming need to be revisited. Its close to Humans. This time the evaluation of Tools should be on **able** shoulders. Meaning, organizations should get them evaluated by **competent** Engineers.

Speaking from my own experience with a team that evaluated Telelogic Tools in one of my past organisation, the reason quoted was, **"Tool generates lot of non readable code"**. My question is do you read the **assembly code generated by C compiler in intermediate stages before generating executable??**

Pessimistic will always be pessimistic. No matter what!! They objected while transitioning from **Assembly to C**. They will object **now** as well. **People** calling **shots**, this time ask for **quantified** evaluation report which should tell "Why Organization should not adopt the given Visual Programming Aid".

I am sure a day will come when there will be speech to Visual Program generator. Visual Program in turn generating the code. Evolution is natural. **Naysayers will make way for competent Engineers in future.**

13

Databases

F ollowing book gives concepts of database systems in general.

1. Database Systems A Pragmatic Approach Elvis C. Foster With Shripad Godbole
2. Database System Concepts Seventh Edition by Avi Silberschatz, Henry F. Korth and S. Sudarshan

For particular flavor of relational data bases such as PostgreSQL, MySQL, MySQL or NoSQL such as MongoDB you could refer respective books. I particularly find the following to the point tutorials from TutorialsPoint very convenient for introductory concepts:

1. SQL TUTORIAL Simply Easy Learning by tutorialspoint.com
2. Similar material you should be able to find for MongoDB and others.

14

Utilities

Any Tool which assists you in development and/or testing is utility. For large C/C++ projects, tools which assist in building, linting, checking memory leaks, assisting in debugging, code formatting, version control are utilities. Integrated Development Platforms or IDE in short are meant to give one stop solution for all these. Then there are testing unit testing tools which are also integrated with IDE in few cases. Your IDE your choice. Some of the IDE that I have used are:

Visual Source Code with its extensions.

Eclipse and Spring Tool Suite.

PyCharm, IntelliJ and Spyder more at https://docs.spyder-ide.org/

15

Data Structure and Algorithms

T his is age old topic with enough good material already available on the web. This book does not want to replicate the material already documented .https://github.com/Abhinandan1414/DataStructuresA ndAlgorithms makes an effort to collate the material already available on the net. The README.md is replicated here.

This is an effort to collate some good material already present.

1. https://www.cs.usfca.edu/~galles/visualization/java/download.html
2. https://algorithm-visualizer.org/
3. https://visualgo.net/en

Reference Books

1. Peter Drake, Data Structures and Algorithms in JAVA
2. S. Dasgupta, C. H. Papadimitriou, and U. V. Vazirani 'Algorithms - Mathematics & Computer Science.pdf'
3. Robert Lafore 'Data Structures and Algorithms in Java.pdf' 5 Michael T. Goodrich, 'Data Structures and Algorithms in Python.pdf'

4. Michael T. Goodrich, 'Data Structures and Algorithms in Java, 6th Edition, 2014.pdf'

Similar Books you should find for Python, C++, Go and Rust

What is the contribution of the Repository

Prof. David Galles,Computer Science, Univerisity of San Francisco has provided the download in the path [1] as Source code: projects.tar.gz. However if you want to build the projects on your own **refactoring** is needed. This repository does that

How to use this Repository?

1. Clone the Repository.
2. Go to cd ds/main you will see build.xml and execute.sh
3. At the Linux command prompt type chmod 755 execute.sh
4. Ensure that Apache Ant is installed in the system.
5. At the Linux command prompt type ./execute.sh You are done!!

Alter/modify the Algorithms as per your study purpose

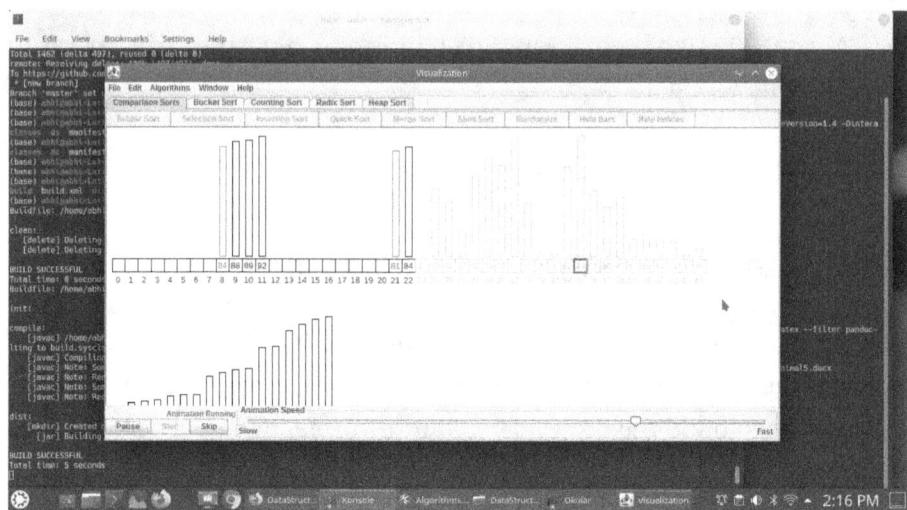

Visualiser In Action

16

Data Formats

D ata Formats is for storing data. Also used for transferring data using suitable communication protocol between end points. Few data formats are JSON, XML, YML etc. JSON is defacto language for modern applications for good reason.

17

Data Analytics and Data Science

While Data Analytics is analyzing the data, Data Science comprises of Machine Learning and Data Engineering.

1. Python Data Analytics With Pandas, NumPy,and Matplotlib Second Edition Fabio Nelli
2. Python Data Science Handbook by Jake VanderPlas
3. Data Science from Scratch by Joel Grus
4. Python for Data Analysis by Wes McKinney
5. Introducing Data Science big data, machine learning,and more, using python tools by Davy Cielen, Arno d. b. Meysman, Mohamed Ali

18

Scientific software

Scientific study involves Mathematics. Sage can be used mathematics related operations. Sage for Undergraduates Book by Gregory V. Bard demonstrates what sage can do. Book by Zimmerman et al. on Sage is also good book.

You could use Python+Scipy+Sympy, Julia, Scilab, Octave, Matlab as an aids for Scientific Study. Scipy has rich documentation including Scipy lecture notes. Sympy documentation is equally useful.

I have Book with the title

1. Mathematics with Sympy, Scipy and Python which is available in all leading Book Stores
2. Course with similar title is available in Udemy

19

Design Tools

Visual Paradigm can be used for Use case, sequence, class, state transition diagrams. Lucid chart is good option for Architecture diagrams. Dia Diagram Editor is an open source option for diagrams.

20

Productivity Tools

Example LibreOffice and Microsoft Office suite of Tools. Libreoffice comes with Writer, Draw,Impress(Presentation) and Calc(Spreadsheet). Similarly Microsoft offers Word,Excel, PowerPoint. For writing, some organizations may be using old word processors such as Latex in such cases you could use Lyx which is what you see is what you get editor. Still better you could use Reedsy for Book writing. For Mathematics intensive content Mathcha editor is excellent choice. Of late lot of support is provided in Microsoft Word thus scientific and research community is not forced to use Tex/Latex. Katex and MathJax need particular mention for Math content.

Case study:

Typora + MathJax, Mathcha editor, MSWord are making Mathematics Academic writing fun.

Also, **markdown** has come such a long way. Create a Book in Typora with markdown and see your self.

Check out this Article "**Typora: You Probably Don't Need a LaTeX Editor**" https://medium.com/@arealguru/you-probably-dont-need-to-be-using-latex-c1483da05e60

21

Project Specific Tools

Your project could be making use of Proprietary Project/Test Management Tools. Please check which Continuous Integration and Continuous Deployment frame work the organization makes use of and which version control system is employed. Which cloud is cloud of choice. Project could be making use of Tools such as MSTeam, Meet, Skype, Zoom etc and most importantly **emails** for communication.

II

Web Development and Web Testing

This section is dedicated for web development and web testing

22

Web Development and Mobile App Development

This is very vast topic. People use JavaScript for front end(Angular, React, Vue). Java(Spring boot), Python (Flask, Django), Rust, JavaScript, Golang as server side programming. Plus various data bases such as SQL and NoSQL. And their various permutation and combinations.

Developers develop mobile application using various implementation languages such Kotlin on Android. The applications could be Native, Web or Hybrid. There is new movement to use Flutter platform. Which promises same code base for Mobile(Android and iOS), Web and Desktop.

Then there is no code/ low code motion by Bubble, Joget, Kissflow, Word-press. Have a look at the following links:

1. https://www.simbla.com/
2. https://www.wix.com
3. https://thunkable.com
4. https://vaadin.com/designer
5. https://bootstrapstudio.io/

Many many more.

There are Books in higher triple digits.

23

Web and Mobile Testing

1. Introduction

B elow is the Test Process document that was prepared for an undisclosed organization which was JavaScript heavy in web development.

Testing Process is supposed to be a live document which outlines Vision, Approach, Implementation, Tools for realizing the Quality Deliverable.

- **The Vision:** The Vision is " To deliver defect free software"
- **The Approach:** To have quality gates at each step to achieve the Vision
- **Implementation:** In letter and spirit the recommendations are implemented in projects/deliverable.
- **Tools:** Employed as necessary to suit the projects need.
- **Quality Deliverable:** End products following Vision, Approach, Implementation and Tools

2. Testing Levels and Types of Testing

Two prevailing models of software development are V model and Iterative model. Iterative or incremental development model consists of large number of iterations where each iteration is complete development loop resulting in a release. Agile and Rapid Application Development are two examples of iterative model. Unlike waterfall model Agile is "Testing through out the software life cycle approach". The software testing consists of various levels. And they are as follows:

- Static testing consisting of review, inspection etc.
- Unit testing
- Component testing
- Integration testing
- System testing

Acceptance testing (In some projects it can be at the end of the project)

This document refers to various testing levels as quality gates. The purpose of each gate is to stop defects percolating to next step. The Cost Of Poor Quality (COPQ) is related to effectiveness in containing the defects in early gates.

Fig gives types of testing. As can be seen from the diagram there are Static (Inspection, Review) and Dynamic (Functional and Non Functional) testing types. Section 3. discusses about Approach and Section 4 Tools and Section 5 talks about deliverable.

Types of Software Testing:

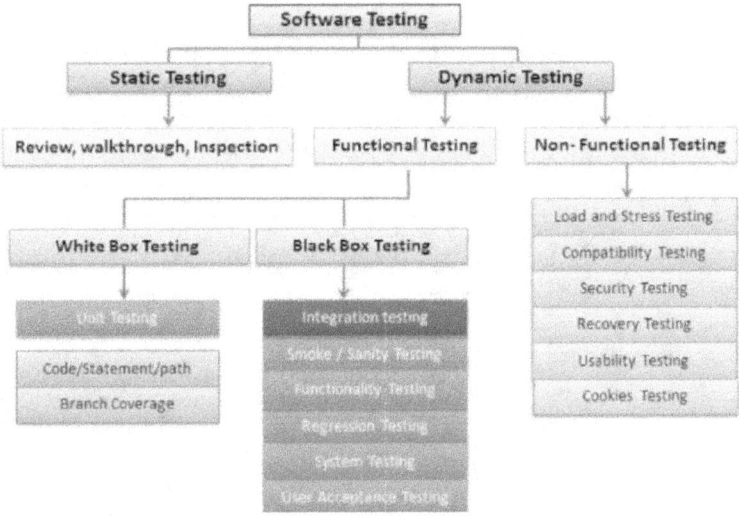

Types of Software Testing

3. Approach of Testing

The idea is to employ as many testing types as possible with sole motto "Defect free software"

- Every team member must know that testing is collective responsibility
- Testable user stories are written with collaboration of developer
- The purpose of continuous development/integration must be understood
- Iteration and release planning difference must be well understood
- Team member must be aware of Tools and Techniques used
- Team member must be aware of the role of automation, mainly in Regression testing

4. Tools for Achieving the End Results

Following table gives the types of testing and Tools that can be use to achieve the motto "Bug free software". **Typo below it is Jest and not Zest**

Type of Testing	Tool Example	Comments
Static testing	Review, Inspection, walk through	Mandatory
Unit testing	Zest, Karma+Jasmine frame work	The tools are specific to JavaScript projects
Code Coverage	Zest	The tool is specific to JavaScript
Functional testing	TestCafeStudio + TestCafe	Should work for any Web/Mobility project
Load+Stress+ Performance	JMeter	Should work for any Web/Mobility project
Security	Sonarqube	Static web testing tool. Works for various programming languages

Example Tool Sets

Functionality testing could also be achieved using Katalon Studio, Cypress and many more tools.

5. Quality Deliverable

The final deliverable is Defect free software which is inline with the motto/philosophy of the Quality initiative.

Summary

Teams shall collectively own the quality of deliverable and shall strive for achieving the motto "Defect free" software. This document shall strive to be reference document for achieving the end goals.

Two good books for security testing related aspects.

1. Hacking. Computer hacking, security testing, penetration testing and Basic security by **Gary Hall and Erin Watson**
2. Mastering Kali Linux for web Penetration Testing by **Michael McPhee**

III

Software Architecture and Design

This section is dedicated for software architecture and software design

24

Software Architecture and Design

1. Software Architecture for Developers by Simon Brown (Must have)
2. Software Architecture in Practice by Len Bass (Must have)
3. Essential Software Architecture Ian Gorton

1 and 2 are must have.

IV

Machine Learning and Deep Learning

This section is for Machine Learning. Rather than trying to write static content, the Author prefers to keep this section live. He uses https://abhinandanhpatil.info to blog regularly on the Machine Learning and Deep Learning findings. The Blog is open to public.

25

Introduction to Machine Learning and Deep Learning

You could start learning Machine Learning and Deep Learning with online courses including Udemy A-Z courses on Machine Learning and Deep Learning by Super Data Science or by 365 Data Science.. As reference books you could have

1. Hands-On Machine Learning with Scikit-Learn and TensorFlow by Aurelian Geron
2. Python Machine Learning By Sebastian Raschka, Vahid Mirjalili
3. The Hundred Page Machine Learning by Burkov
4. Introduction to Machine Learning by Alex Smola and Vishwanathan
5. Deep Learning by Ian, Yoshua and Aaron
6. Mastering Machine Learning with Python in Six Steps by Manohar-Swamynathan

Some of the Machine Learning packages include

1. Scikit learn
2. Keras+Tensorflow

3. JASP and Orange3 for visual programming

For Mathematics background you can refer

1. Mathematics for machine learning book (Book by A. Aldo Faisal, Cheng Soon Ong, and Marc Peter Deisenroth).

Many good courses in Udemy for Machine Learning and Deep Learning.

State of the Art of Machine Learning and Deep Learning

JAVA and ML
1) Weka snapshot 3.9.5 https://www.cs.waikato.ac.nz/ml/weka/, go for daily snapshot builds.
2) DL4J 1.0.0.Beta6 (7 is expected) https://deeplearning4j.org/, DL4J continues stay relevant with lots of examples
3) https://github.com/awslabs/djl

Python and ML
1) To begin with any decent Udemy A Z machine Learning github repository
2) Any Udemy A Z Deep Learning github repository
3) https://github.com/amueller/introduction_to_ml_with_python // Very good image processing examples
4) https://github.com/scikit-learn/scikit-learn.git //One stop for all the ML Learning needs of Python
5) https://github.com/keras-team/keras // Deep learning needs
6) Supporting matplotlib

Julia and ML
1) https://github.com/denizyuret/Knet.jl //Looking very promising
2) https://github.com/FluxML/Flux.jl

Visual Programming for ML

1) Orange Resources https://github.com/biolab?q=orange3-

2) Deep Learning Studio https://deepcognition.ai/

General expectation of mine: Machine Learning/Deep Learning is inter disciplinary learning involving Mathematics, Statistics and Software Engineering. People(Data Scientists) should not be spending lot of time in coding and re-inventing wheel every time. Rather there are many domain specific problems which they can concentrate on. BTW, is there any domain where ML/DL is not relevant? Starting from Agriculture to Healthcare. From General governance to Corporate governance. Sky is the limit.

27

Selected Content from
https://14inc.ltd/blog-feed/

Hello PyTorch!!

h ttps://pytorch.org/
I spent some time reading every bit on this page. The philosophy of PyTorch echoes with my requirements. Last time I had just cloned the examples directory without reading the main page of PyTorch. i.e I did:

~/MyLearning/Python/PyTorchExamples$ find ./ –name "." –print | wc -1

120

Too **small** number for this capable library.

This misled me. I will be spending some **" more"** time **"learning"** about **PyTorch**

Deep Learning Libraries Need to be More Intelligent

Only there are three vital parameters. Processing power(CPU+GPU), Primary Memory and Disk access latency. Talking about Processing Power and Primary Memory, can't Deep Learning libraries **query** that on their own? For example, DL4J is able to do that to some extent. It is evident:

o.n.l.f.Nd4jBackend – Loaded [CpuBackend] backend
o.n.n.NativeOpsHolder – Number of threads used for linear algebra: 2
o.n.n.Nd4jBlas – Number of threads used for OpenMP BLAS: 2
o.n.l.a.o.e.DefaultOpExecutioner – Backend used: [CPU]; OS: [Linux]
o.n.l.a.o.e.DefaultOpExecutioner – **Cores: [4]; Memory: [2.0GB];**
o.n.l.a.o.e.DefaultOpExecutioner – Blas vendor: [OPENBLAS]

This is on cluster. Still Dl4J is not able to make full use of Memory. On the other hand **not so intelligent** libraries like **TensorFlow** are relying on user to set them. **Configurable parameters** in general should be bare **minimal**

You have only two parameters Processing Power + Memory and they should be set to **max available**.

In my case, I am able to use the partial processing power of cluster. Even programming languages can become more intelligent. Including JAVA. I should **not** be setting alias **java="java -Xms1G -Xmx2G -Dorg.bytedeco.javacpp.maxbytes=4G**

-Dorg.bytedeco.javacpp.maxphysicalbytes=6G". Intelligence should be built every where Libraries and Programming alike. Intelligence everywhere.

One more thing: Few libraries are using CUDA meant for proprietary GPU namely NVIDIA Graphics card. It is against the **foundation principle** of AI/ML/DL. Libraries are meant to be **open and democratic.** Should work on AMD, Intel **"including"** NVIDIA.

Mother of All Comparison DL4J vs PyTorch vs TensorFlow vs Theano with CNN

I do not belong to sales department of any of the Libraries. Just want to tell the truth.

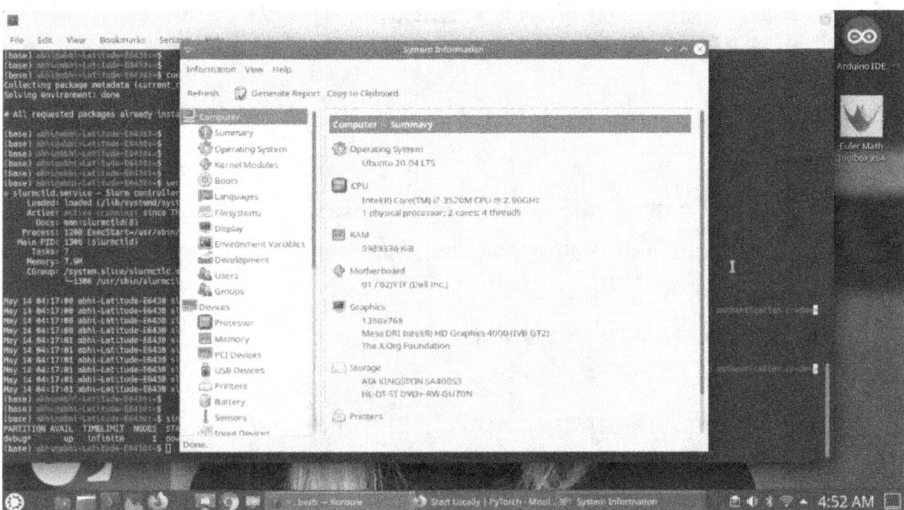

MNIST CNN

Library	CPU Max	Mem Max	Time+ in Top to reach 98% Acc
PyTorch	299%	**6.8%**	13:59
TensorFlow	**400%+**	**14.9%**	**29:02**
Theano	**201%**	12.2%	9:44
DL4J	295%	10.2%	**4:14**

MNIST CNN

Observations:

1. DL4J fastest to reach 98% Accuracy
2. Theano lightest on CPU
3. PyTorch lightest on Memory
4. **TensorFlow Worst with respect to CPU, Memory and slowest to reach 98% Accuracy**

Learning:

1. **Do NOT go by installation size of the library**
2. **Industry requirements for employment and crowd need not be correct always**
3. **Top utility rocks. Even after so many years.**

PyTorch+Scripts are smart enough to make use of Docker swarm environment and bring down the execution time.

Full Credits to PyTorch, Docker Swarm, PyTorch Scripts and important Continuumio for providing required Docker support.

Full credits to **Canonical** for providing the required infrastructure https://blog.ruanbekker.com/blog/2019/01/10/ setup-a-3-node-docker-swarm-cluster-on-ubuntu-16-dot-04/ Got me interested in forming 3 node docker swarm.

Further I wanted to evaluate how much the available DeepLearning Libraries are able to utilise the infrastructure.

I created the three node docker swarm using the concept mentioned in the blog however deviated in deploying the docker image.

At the heart lies the command

docker run -t -i continuumio/anaconda3 /bin/bash (Credits to Continuumio for this)

This command takes the Docker image anaconda3 and most important gives the access to /bin/bash. After that it is regular Scripts execution without modifying single line of the Scripts. Significant deviation from Spark approach. Where you have to modify the scripts and use PySpark.

The git clone https://github.com/pytorch/examples gives rich set of scripts. I took regular mnist_cnn.py example. Here is what I noticed.

1) regular script execution would have taken 39:16 Time+(TOP) with 300% CPU utilisation at the end of 3rd Epoch

2) With Docker Swarm it was brought down to 15:26 Time+(TOP) with mere 194% CPU utilisation at the end of 3rd Epoch by off loading some work to compute nodes.

Summary: PyTorch is smart enough to bring down Time+(TOP) drastically with 30% reduction in CPU usage in the controller node and delegates the CPU work to compute nodes.

Further, the PyTorch brought down to the 38% execution time with Docker swarm in anaconda3 environment.

Docker Swarm consits of
abhi-Latitude-E6430 Ready Active Leader 19.03.8
abhi-HP-EliteBook-840-G2 Ready Active 19.03.8
abhi-Lenovo-ideapad-330-15IKB Ready Active 19.03.8

Thank You for Introducing me to Orange

Credits: https://analyticsindiamag.com/
5-open-source-ml-tools-you-can-use-without-coding/
I am using Orange from morning and my curiosity is growing by hour.
Resources https://github.com/biolab?q=orange3-
I am also trying to learn Deep Learning Studio https://deepcognition.ai/
If you are a developer you may want to check out https://www.fluidstack.io/

Back to Basics Again, This Time with Orange3

OpenML Electricity DataSet. Number of Instances **45312**.

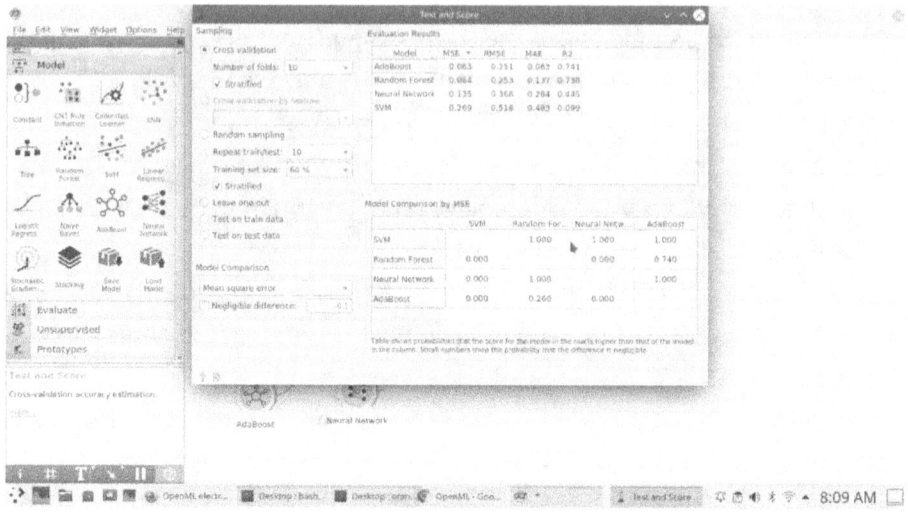

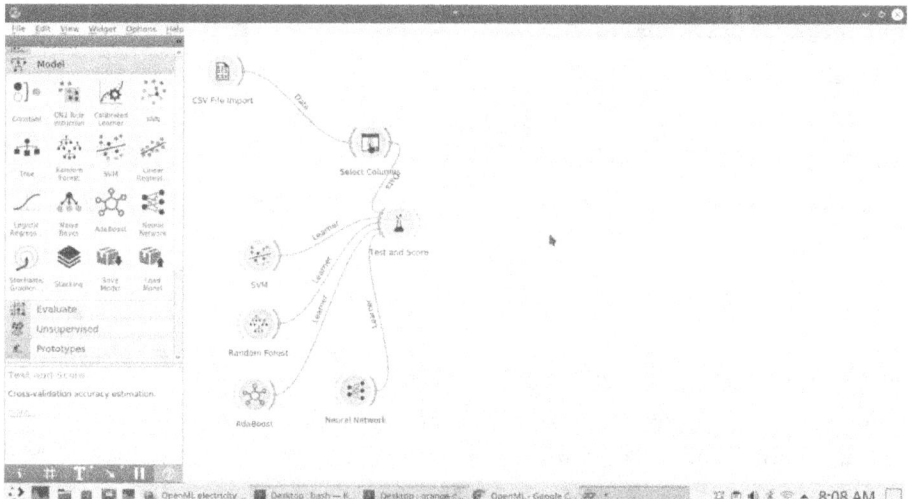

And we were always told Neural Networks are best for large data sets.

Inception V3/ VGG 16

https://youtu.be/9SjBT4i1-bA

LOW CODE APPROACH TO MACHINE LEARNING

Low code approach using Wrapper around proven **Sci-kit Learn** and others.

1) git clone the repository **pycaret**

2) Since I am using Conda environment, some of the requirements are not met. Missing packages in Conda and Conda-Forge can be found using »conda install -y -q -c conda-forge −file requirements.txt

cufflinks

kmodes

datefinder

yellowbrick

datetime

3) Set the pycaret env using conda

4) conda install -c conda-forge jupyterlab

5) pip3 install −extra-index-url https://pypi.anaconda.org/Abhinandan1414 /simple pycaret

6) Enable notebook extension as per your choice: TabNine, Hinterland or treetab or refer https://github.com/Jupyter-contrib/jupyter_nbextensions_ configurator

```
Out[8]:
```

	Model	MAE	MSE	RMSE	R2	RMSLE	MAPE
0	CatBoost Regressor	683.624800	1985415.174000	1388.247100	0.980100	0.072900	0.053900
1	Light Gradient Boosting Machine	759.132400	2863935.679300	1643.467700	0.972600	0.079400	0.058100
2	Huber Regressor	921.968700	3436964.447100	1837.119200	0.975000	0.095800	0.070000
3	Random Forest	858.166000	3508114.317300	1837.629100	0.965400	0.090900	0.066300
4	Ridge Regression	932.424600	3559808.678400	1865.617000	0.965000	0.095600	0.070700
5	Random Sample Consensus	937.531900	3644070.978400	1886.607700	0.964000	0.095600	0.070700
6	Support Vector Machine	868.462300	3667101.469700	1884.777000	0.963900	0.086600	0.063200
7	Bayesian Ridge	936.351400	3672909.674400	1892.017100	0.963800	0.095600	0.070700
8	Linear Regression	938.564400	3678094.047600	1895.372500	0.963700	0.095600	0.070800
9	Least Angle Regression	997.935500	4533390.638800	2084.082600	0.955400	0.106600	0.074700
10	Extra Trees Regressor	959.806500	4595932.264100	2076.155300	0.955300	0.104700	0.075400
11	Decision Tree	982.447100	4765994.268900	2123.042600	0.953700	0.107500	0.076900
12	Gradient Boosting Regressor	1119.090900	5070620.280600	2207.484400	0.950400	0.111800	0.084300
13	Passive Aggressive Regressor	1184.734900	5475692.120600	2240.859300	0.948500	0.118200	0.089200
14	Extreme Gradient Boosting	1130.885300	5376247.006800	2263.830400	0.947600	0.112500	0.084900
15	TheilSen Regressor	1428.979600	14005359.316700	3677.001000	0.865400	0.155100	0.094900
16	K Neighbors Regressor	3297.595900	43143598.456100	6526.761100	0.573700	0.398000	0.262300

V

Internet of Things

This section introduces readers to Internet of Things

28

Internet of Things

For introduction to IoT you could refer:

1. The Intenet of Things: Do it yourself projects by Donald Norris
2. Intenet of Things (IoT) Technologies, Applications, Challenges, and Solutions CRC Press
3. Internet-of-Things (IoT) Systems by Dimitrios Serpanos and Marilyn Wolf
4. Internet of Things: A Hands-on Approach Book by Arshdeep Bahga and Vijay K. Madisetti

For support of IoT in cloud one can refer respective cloud service provider documents:

1. https://azure.microsoft.com/en-in/solutions/architecture/azure-iot-s ubsystems/
2. AWS IoT Developers Guide available at AWS

Summary: Cloud service providers have frame-work in place for Internet of Things Developers which they can readily make use of.

VI

Cloud from User's perspective

29

Cloud from Users Perspective

Talking in particular about AWS there are courses for various levels:

1. AWS Cloud Practitioner
2. AWS Developer
3. AWS Certified Solutions Architect
4. AWS SysOps Administrator

For example on Udemy you can take courses which are aligned for them. For example I have taken AWS Certified (Solutions Architect, Developer, SysOps Administrator, Cloud Practitioner) which is four in one course. Few noteworthy documents follow:

1. AWS General Reference, Reference Guide, https://docs.aws.amazon.com /general/latest/gr/aws-general.pdf
2. Fundamentals of Azure, Microsoft Azure essentials available at Microsoft
3. https://cloud.google.com/docs/overview for Google Cloud

Summary: Every cloud service provider supplements the cloud services with user guide which can be used on the need basis.

VII

Block Chain

30

Block Chain

31

Blockchain and its Applications

ollowing book can be referred:

1. Blockchain Enabled Applications by Vikram Dhillon David Metcalf Max Hooper
2. BlockChain Revolution by Don Tapscott
3. Hands-On Blockchain with Hyperledger Nitin Gaur Luc Desrosiers Venkatraman Ramakrishna et al.
4. Mastering Bitcoin Programming the Open Blockchain Andreas M. Antonopoulos
5. Blockchain Applications: A Hands-On Approach by Arshdeep Bagha and Vijay Madisetti

VIII

Process Related

32

What is Process in Software Industry

P rocess is best practices which continuously evolve. Consult your organizations process repository, intranet, experts to get more insights for process tailor made for your organization.

1. Software Engineering: A Practitioner's Approach Book by Roger S. Pressman

IX

DevOps

33

DevOPs

D evOPs is rather philosophy where Development and Operations Team work in Unison to ensure hassle free delivery. DevOPs is particularly attractive for companies which are mainly into Web and Mobile App development using Agile and SCRUM methodology. Plenty of teaching material on Web including free YouTube contents on this topic are available.

X

Microcontrollers and Hardware

34

MicroControllers and Electronics

Some great resources for Microcontroller and Embedded Systems Books are as follows:

1. Embedded Systems Volume 1,2,3 by Jonathan W. Valvano
2. Fast and Effective Embedded Systems Design by Rob Toulson Tim Wilmshurst
3. The Definitive Guide to ARM Cortex -M3 and Cortex-M4 Processors Third Edition Joseph Yiu

For Electronics Knowledge of Peripheral Devices:

1. Electronics Cookbook Practical Electronic Recipes with Arduino and Raspberry Pi Simon Monk
2. Electronics Fundamentals Circuits, Devices and Applications Thomas L. Floyd David L. Buchla Eighth Edition
3. Digital Electronics Principles, Devices and Applications Anil K. Maini

XI

Robotics

35

Robotics

Robotics is very vast field. However for students learning Robotics with initial steps to get the feel of Robotics:

1. Beginning Robotics with Raspberry Pi and Arduino Using Python and OpenCV Jeff Cicolani

XII

Industry 4.0

36

Industry 4.0

A lready many enterprises are in Industry 3.0 where they are making use of ICT enabled solutions. In Industry 4.0, Automation, Smart Machines and Smart Factories will rule. That is Operation Technology (Real World) and Information Technology (Digital world) will work in Tandem and Unison. Which also means:

1. Cloud Technologies
2. IIoT
3. Security
4. AI/ML/DL/DS/Analytics
5. 5G and Edge Computing

Will all work together to make infinite possibilities with infinite data. Few Enterprises already working on Digital Enterprises.

XIII

Quantum Computing

37

Quantum Computing

I s very niche field with few players as of now:

1. Practical Quantum Computing for Developers by Vladimir Silva
2. Quantum Computation and Quantum Information by Michael A. Nielsen & Isaac L. Chuang
3. Quantum computing for computer scientists Noson S. Yanofsky and Mirco A. Mannucci

XIV

Sun Rise Sectors

38

SUN Rise or Promising Sectors

Predicting tech shift in coming years is always difficult; **Here are my Big 5.**

- Renewable Energy
- Digital Transformative Technologies
- Cooling Technology
- Private investment in Aerospace Sectors
- Private Investment in Defense Sectors

All these sectors are STEM dependent. M as in Mathematics. Which means reskilling or upskilling the tech work force.

XV

Intangible Skills

39

Valuable Assets aka Intangible Skills

Intangible skills include but not limited to Intelligence Quotient, Emotional Quotient, Language Proficiency, Communication skills, Aptitude and Attitude, Team membership and most importantly Ethics and Integrity

Conclusion

This book makes an attempt to serve as reference material for essential skills required by **new** software professionals.

About the Author

Abhinandan is Author of 10 Technology Books and 14 Scientific Articles in Journals. Before this, he has worked in Wireless Network Software Organization as Lead Software Engineer for close to a decade. Abhinandan was in USA for two long stints and was instrumental in Releases of Mobility Manager at Motorola USA as Single Point of Contact for Network Simulator Tool. His Research is available as Books and Thesis in IJSER, USA. His Thesis published as Book is rated as one of the best Books of all time for Regression testing by BookAuthority.org. Awarded RULA Award for the same Thesis in 2019. He is Active Researcher in the field of Machine Learning, Deep Learning, Data Science, Artificial Intelligence, Regression Testing applied to Networks, Communication and Internet of Things. He is active contributor of Science, Technology, Engineering and Mathematics. He is currently working on few Undisclosed Books. He has started Blogging recently on Technology and Allied Areas. He is a RULA Research Awardee in 2019. He is Adarsh Vidya Saraswati Rashtriya Puraskar Awardee in year 2020. Abhinandan is Senior IEEE member since 2013 and is member of Smart Tribe and Cheeky Scientists Association. He also holds mini MBA from IBMI, Germany. UGC-NET Qualified (2012). Recipient of several Bravo awards for deserving work at Motorola. He is on the Editorial Board of few Scientific Journals. Dr. Patil is an ardent reader of STEM(Science, Technology, Engineering and Mathematics). He has a desire to contribute more to STEM.

You can connect with me on:

🌐 https://abhinandanhpatil.info

f https://www.facebook.com/abhinandan.h.patil

🔗 https://in.linkedin.com/in/abhinandan-h-patil

Also by Abhinandan H Patil

In-addition to the Papers and Thesis in leading Journals, My published work as Books is available online

1. Design and Implementation of Combinatorial Testing based Test suites for Operating Systems used for Internet of Things

2. Enhancement of CodeCover Tool for JAVA Projects

3. Regression Testing in Era of Internet of Things and Machine Learning: A practical approach

4. Essential Skills for Software Engineers

5. Computer System Performance Analysis an Informal Approach

6. Mathematics Part 1

7. Software Engineering for Communication Network Engineers

8. Mathematics Part 6: Mathematics Learning with Aid of Software

9. Evolution of Computing: From Logic Gates to Parallel Computers and Beyond

10. Quantitative Methods with Python